Presented To:

_____

From:

_____

Date:

_____

BURNING ONES

DESTINY IMAGE BOOKS BY JERAME NELSON

Manifesting God's Love Through Signs, Wonders, and Miracles:
Discovering the Keys to the Kingdom

BURNING ONES

CALLING FORTH
A GENERATION OF
DREAD CHAMPIONS

JERAME NELSON

DESTINY IMAGE® PUBLISHERS, INC.

P.O. Box 310, Shippensburg, PA 17257-0310

"Promoting Inspired Lives"

This book and all other Destiny Image, Revival Press, MercyPlace, Fresh Bread, Destiny Image Fiction, and Treasure House books are available at Christian bookstores and distributors worldwide.

For a U.S. bookstore nearest you, call **1-800-722-6774.**

For more information on foreign distributors, call **717-532-3040.**

Reach us on the Internet: **www.destinyimage.com.**

ISBN 13 TP: 978-0-7684-4008-9

ISBN 13 Ebook: 978-0-7684-8926-2

For Worldwide Distribution, Printed in the U.S.A.

1 2 3 4 5 6 7 8 9 10 11 / 13 12 11

ENDORSEMENTS

I believe God wants to release in the earth what Isaiah saw in his throne room encounter, burning ones who live in the presence of the King and boldly declare the glory of God filling the earth that releases a flood of His presence in cities and nations. Jerame Nelson's *Burning Ones* calls us to be those who are consumed by God's presence and declare His goodness in the earth through radical love and raw power. My prayer is that this book will ignite within you a fire that will result in entire cities saved and nations transformed.

Banning Liebscher
Director, Jesus Culture
Author, *Jesus Culture: Living a Life That Transforms the World*

It is with enthusiasm and confidence that I recommend Jerame Nelson and his book, *Burning Ones*. I have watched Jerame develop in his walk with the Lord over the last several years and observed his commitment to integrity, humility, and Christlikeness. All of those attributes and more are woven into his new book and imparted through the truths he has captured. Clearly, this is a new generation with a fresh mandate coming straight from God's heart. Because of the uniqueness of our generational calling, supernatural passion and spiritual fire are essential attributes to become one of God's champions. Jerame has done an excellent job of communicating these traits and how to obtain them while at the same time encouraging us to press into the intimacy and fellowship with the Lord where our flaming hearts are ignited. I believe you will not only enjoy this book, but also be mobilized into your personal calling and destiny through the anointing resident on it.

Paul Keith Davis
WhiteDove Ministries
Orange Beach, Alabama

In the *Burning Ones,* my good friend Jerame Nelson accurately articulates God's heart and mind regarding His revolutionary love—an irresistible power to capture the hearts of the unchurched as well as empower you to reach your highest potential as a son or daughter of God. This God-ordained book will drive a greater spirit fervor into your heart and give you the awakening into the unquenchable inner passions that you've been longing for! Jerame's unique writing style, humor, spiritual encounters, and personal experiences that are revealed in this book both equip and challenge you to live as a contagious Burning One.

Tracey Armstrong
Best-Selling Author, *Followership*
Founder, Citadel Churches

Contents

FOREWORD BY
JAMES W. GOLL

Dread Champions are forerunners who prepare the way with a blazing message from God in their generation. They are a light shining brightly in a lost world with a calling to penetrate this temporary present darkness. They have oil in their lamps and are prepared for whatever comes their way.

They are history-makers and culture-changers. They are radical disciples of the one who radically loves them. They are laid-down lovers. They are ordinary people who do extraordinary exploits by being empowered by a present-tense relationship with the original Burning One. Burning Ones burn with the love of God.

In February 2009, I was helping host a gathering called "*I must burn!*" It was 72 hours of nonstop worship and prayer hosted at a wonderful presence-based church. We had teaching and ministry times interspersed in between the worship sets.

I was to minister at the 70th-hour slot, and I was captured by His presence. The place was saturated with the living, breathing presence of the Almighty!

I was teaching, singing, praying, and prophesying, weaving in and out of different waves of the Holy Spirit as they came crashing in on the scene. I got stuck on a phrase, and it has been stuck in me ever since. I kept saying and singing, *"Make me a lamp burning in my generation."* Ever since then, like a broken record, I get caught in a phrase and often repeat it over and over and over.

"Give me oil in my lamp, keep me burning, burning, burning. Give me oil in my lamp, I pray. Give me oil in my lamp, keep me burning, burning, burning. Keep me burning till the break of day."

Do you want to be a Burning One?

Burning Ones have their lamps filled with the oil of intimacy with their Master. Burning Ones walk so closely with Jesus that they only cast one shadow. Burning Ones are consumed with their message. But they are not driven. They are consumed. They come to an end of themselves along the pathway of becoming, and the message and the messenger have become one.

Wow!

Do you long to be consumed with the fire of His love? I do!

You are holding in your hands a book from a young trailblazer who longs for the supernatural fruit of the Spirit in his life as much he longs for the supernatural display of the Holy

Spirit's power. Dread Champions are not born. Dread Champions are formed!

No matter your background, no matter your ethnic origin or income level, God is an equal opportunity employer. He is looking for abandoned men and women who want the fame of His name to be spread through their sphere of influence.

It is my pleasure and delight to commend to you the life, ministry, and now the writings of one of God's fresh young generals in this generation. Listen to his plea. Jerame Nelson will help you to catch the fire that will not burn out.

Do you want to be a Burning One?

Then read on!

James W. Goll
Encounters Network
Prayer Storm
Compassion Acts
Author, *The Seer, The Call to the Elijah Generation, Dream Language, Prayer Storm, The Lost Art of Intercession,* and many others
www.jamesgoll.com

INTRODUCTION

I believe that God is raising up the Burning Ones in this hour. Their hearts will burn for the lost. They will long to see the mandate of the Great Commission of God fulfilled. They will carry the fire of God's love and compassion for people and be willing to step out of their comfort zones to minister to others. They will burn for Jesus, and others will take note.

John the Baptist was a Burning One. John was a *voice* crying out in the wilderness sent by God to prepare the way of the Lord. All of Judea and the surrounding regions of the Jordan heard his voice and came out to be baptized by him for the remission of sins (see Matt. 3:2-5). They knew John's reputation of being a fiery prophet who was known and even feared by the religious leaders of his day. Even Jesus held John in high regard, calling John *"the burning and shining lamp"* drawing people who came to the light of his burning for God (John 5:35). John caught fire for God. Everything he said and did spoke of the redeeming love of the Father. He wasn't afraid to be seen and heard.

Jesus too, was a burning and shining lamp in His time and day. The Bible says that entire villages and towns would come out to hear Him preach words they had never heard preached before and to receive miracles from God. He was the most loved and hated person on the planet—and still is. Those in gross darkness and sin loved Him, and those who were religious hated Him, yet could not say or do anything to Him because of His popularity with the people of His day. Everywhere Jesus went, He was a bright and shining lamp showing the glory of God through signs, wonders, and miracles. (See John 1:4-5.)

We are called to be like Jesus and John. God wants us to burn brightly for Him everywhere we go, to be a voice and to reveal His goodness and love to a dying and lost world. Will we be ones who will burn for Jesus, carry the message of His Kingdom, and reveal our Father's love to those around us? Are we ready for a supernatural empowerment to become like Him? We cannot do it in our own strength, but we can position ourselves to become Burning Ones, dread champions of God.

This book is all about helping you position yourself to receive more of God, to embrace the fire, and to begin to burn for God. Are you ready to catch fire and become a Burning One? God is raising up a company of champions who will burn brightly for Him and carry the flames of revival and God's love for all to see. Are you ready to step out and become a dread champion who is burning with the presence and power and love of the Lord? God has a purpose for your life, and it is this: You are His chosen one,

His Burning One, and all of Heaven is focused on you, right now, to see how you will respond to this invitation.

You are invited to become one of the company of Burning Ones who burn with God's fire. Let me show you what this looks like and how it feels to burn. After all, this is a "show me" generation. People no longer want to just hear the words of God; they want to see God in action.

Jesus was a Burning One who was full of action and full of love. Everywhere He went, He lit fires, showing forth the good works of His Father's Kingdom by demonstrating God's power; as a result, the hearts of many were set ablaze. What made Jesus different from all of the other religious leaders of His day was He didn't just talk about God. He demonstrated who God was by releasing the works of God.

God wants to give us tools to release His love, tools like signs, wonders, and miracles, as well as the prophetic, to open the hearts of men and women to receive the great love of our Father. God wants those whose hearts burn for Him to demonstrate His love in action outside of the church.

A Prayer for Healing

One time, as I was shopping at a Guess clothing store in San Diego, California, looking at shirts, I turned around and almost knocked a guy over. As I bumped into him, I couldn't help but notice this huge sling on his arm. It wrapped all the way around his waist and up his chest and then came up and around his shoulder, pinning his arm to his chest.

A normal shopper would have said, "Excuse me," and walked on. A normal Christian may have prayed a brief prayer like, "Oh God, help that guy get his life straight, lead Him to you, and heal him." A Burning One would realize that God was setting the guy up for a divine appointment, an encounter that would change his life. A Burning One sees opportunities to reveal the light everywhere. Burning Ones want to pass on the fire for healing and salvation through a word and a touch. They become emboldened because they are so filled with God, they take no thought for the enemy and do what they are called to do—seek and save the lost, stretch out their hands to heal, release the captives, and be the dread champion warriors of the Kingdom of God they were called to be.

So when I bumped into this guy, I realized that God had set me up and this was a divine appointment.

I asked the young man what happened to him and why he had that huge sling on him. He told me that he was into extreme sports and raced motorcycles. A week before I bumped into him, he went up and over this jump, flew off of his bike, crashed, and tore his rotator cuff in half. He then went on to tell me that the doctors told him and his family that he would have to wear the brace for at least nine months until the rotator cuff could heal right. So after listening, I told him I was a believer in Jesus and asked if I could pray for him to get healed. He ended up saying *yes*, and as I went to lay hands on his shoulder and pray, I noticed that two guys who were homosexual employees working at the store were eavesdropping on our conversation and watching us to see what would happen.

As they stared at us like I was from another world, I prayed a simple prayer for God to heal this young man. After I prayed, I asked the boy if he could feel any difference. He began to try to move his arm in the sling and said, "Actually, there is a difference." Then he told me that his mom had to help him out of bed that morning because he was in such pain due to this injury, but that it felt like it was better.

Then, right there in front of those two store employees, I told the young man, "Why don't you take that huge brace off and see if you are healed?" At first the young man didn't want to do it, but then all of a sudden he just went for it. It took him two minutes to get out of the sling. But once it was off, he threw it on the ground and began swinging his arm all around crying out, "I'm healed! I'm healed!"

The two guys who worked at the store were shocked. The mother of the young man was present, and she was just as shocked. After a few minutes of the young man testing out his arm, I asked him if he knew Jesus, and he told me that he did, so I told him that this miracle was a sign of God's love for him. After that, the boy and his mother left the store full of joy.

I turned around to shop some more and noticed the two workers staring at me as if they were freaked out. I took the opportunity to talk with the two guys and bought a few shirts from them. I didn't try to preach at them or tell them they needed to repent. I just treated them as nicely as I could and left, knowing that a seed of God's love had just been planted in their hearts. We are called to model the love of the Father until others' lives are saved and transformed—not judge them.

Are You Ready to Burn?

I'm burning with the fire of God's love. Are you?

I stepped into the salvation of God and within four years was released to full-time ministry as a Burning One, a revivalist with a mandate in this hour of Church history to call you forth.

We are standing at the edge of a great outpouring of God's love where the knowledge of the glory of the Lord will be known throughout the world. Will you be one who carries that knowledge to the world, one who is a carrier of God's love and power? One who releases miracles of healing or revelation that transform individuals, cities, and even nations? Are you positioned to step into this invitation to become transformed from an ordinary believer to a Burning One empowered by God to seek and save the lost, to undo the works of the enemy, to release healing, miracles, signs, and wonders that cause people to stand up and take notice that the glory of the Lord is being released?

Read on and see how you can become positioned for more.

The first step is to leave your cave of obscurity and insecurity. The second step calls you to embrace the fire of His love and move into an encounter that will transform you completely. It is a calling that leads to a commissioning. An increase of power and love follows. And as you run with Him, roaring with authority and scaling new heights of victory, you will feel His pleasure. His heart will beat with yours. His thoughts will become yours. Come and run with the company of the Burning Ones—bold believers who are feared and loved: feared because of the fire they release, loved because of the heart of the Father evident in their eyes and compassionate touch.

Come on! I'm talking to you!

CHAPTER 1

THE HEART AND MINDSET OF A BURNING ONE

God is raising up a generation of Burning Ones who will be champions of love, and everywhere they go, they will show forth the reality of God's love to people who are lost and hurting. Unfortunately, people have funny ideas about what love looks like. People do all kinds of strange things in the name of the Lord: They scream at the devil, smack people down when they pray for people's healing, get showy and loud, and call it zeal for the Lord. They may be releasing genuine anointing, but really, all they are showing is a total lack of love.

I remember when I first launched out in ministry, zealous for God and zealous to see His power manifest. I was one of the strange ones, thinking I was one of the Burning Ones. When I look back at it now, I wonder what the heck I was thinking.

I remember one time being in a revival meeting in Sacramento, California, and as I stood up to preach, I told those in the room that God had spoken to me that He was going to do creative miracles and heal people who needed miracles in their bodies. God was particularly interested in healing those who had metal surgically implanted into bones that had been broken or shattered in accidents. I gave an altar call for anyone who had metal surgically implanted, and about 11 people walked up to the front.

As I begin to pray, I remember praying for one older lady who had a metal rod in her hip. She could not walk well. Instead of laying hands on her gently and praying, I full on kicked her—really hard—in her hip, three times. She fell on the ground, and God graciously, instantly healed her after I did this. The woman came undone, excited that she could not find the metal rod in her hip anymore. Afterward, 9 out of the 11 people were instantly healed and testified to not being able to find the pins, plates, or screws that had been surgically implanted in their bodies by the doctors.

You might think that sounds odd, kicking an older lady, but I was used to punching, kicking, and smacking people and seeing God do miracles all the time. People never said anything to me because of the results; people would be healed every time. I especially got weird with people who had demons in my meetings. If there was a devil in one of my meetings, I would scream, "Bring that person up here now!" Then I would grab the person by the head and scream at him or her in front of hundreds of people. Oftentimes, the people wouldn't get fully delivered and would have to be dragged off to some back room to be delivered and healed. I used to think that this was the way we were supposed to do ministry. I had read Scriptures like the one out of First John that said that Jesus manifested Himself to destroy the works of the devil, and I took it literally. My mission in life was to destroy the devil. The reality was that I was nothing other than an anointed jerk.

I had zeal without the knowledge of God's love, and because I had a gift of faith and miracles operating in my life, I thought that I was doing the good works of Jesus everywhere I went— until one day God Himself corrected me.

A Message from God

I remember being in a meeting and calling a person up to the platform to cast out a demon, and then I grabbed her by the head in front of this huge crowd and began to scream at her for the demon to come out.

All of a sudden, I heard the Lord say to me, "Son, stop that. Hate the demon, but love the person."

When I heard God say this, I took a step back and said to God, "What?"

He replied, "Why don't you try love? Just wave your hand at her and tell her God loves her and see what happens." So I did just as the Holy Spirit told me, and the woman was instantly delivered. It was the easiest deliverance from a demon I had ever seen.

I realized that making a huge show about casting the devils out of people was insensitive to those people and perhaps even damaged their reputation in front of their entire church family. That day, I started a love journey with God that has resulted in much more consistency of God's power and faith showing up in our meetings today.

At that time I would see strange miracles because I had a gift of faith and healing, but it wasn't always consistent. Sometimes, lots of miracles would break out, and sometimes I would work so hard praying for people and only a few would happen, and I would just think to myself, *Man that was a hard meeting. The enemy has a stronghold here.* But after the Lord spoke to me about loving people, everything changed.

Burning Ones Think Differently About Power and Love...

God wants to change the way we think regarding His power and love. Now that we clearly understand the purpose of God's power—to reveal His goodness and love—we must step into this new way of thinking. What I'm talking about is the mindset of a Burning One. For far too long, people have been living in a place that I like to call "misplaced passion." They are zealous ones, zealous for something they don't understand. Paul talked about people who had zeal for God without knowledge and how it was destructive instead of good (see Rom. 10:2). We are living in a time and a day where people are misrepresenting God the Father all of the time because they don't know God's love.

When I began to change the way I thought about God's power and love and focus on the goodness of God rather than destroying the works of the devil, things really took off for us in our ministry. From that day onward, we consistently began seeing God do creative miracles like the ones you find in the Bible. I have not been to a nation of the earth since that time where we have had a big struggle with seeing miracles, and the reason why is this: I now understand that the miracles are vehicles for people to connect with God's love. I realize now that I don't have to help God out by yelling and doing weird things to see Him do miracles. He wants to do these things because they are signs of His great love toward people.

When you understand this, it will set you free from having to perform for God or other people. It makes this whole miracle thing easy, and it will boil down to the fact that the reason God heals today and wants to heal you is that He wants to reveal His goodness and love through the miracles so people would know that He is a good Father who loves them.

CALLED TO BE DIFFERENT

Do you know His love? Have you encountered Him miraculously, personally, receiving a healing or a prophetic word that changed the direction of your life? Or have you been turned off by odd, zealous "revivalists" who have yet to know God's love, much less reveal it? Rather than judging people who are operating like I once did, recognize that you are free to be different.

God is calling you to be a Burning One—not an idiot.

It is not wrong to be loud or zealous in meetings or in the streets as we share our faith. Just be who you are, and God will show up. If you are loud and full of zeal in your personality, just go for it. Just make sure you add love and make it the first priority to all that you do, and you will be blessed. I am still loud and full of fire, but have added the most important thing, and that is being motivated by love in all that I am doing.

God wants us to understand that if we will just focus on being with Him and catching the fire of His love, we will naturally walk in signs, wonders, and miracles. He wants us to stop having a warrior mentality that's focused on the devil and destroying his Kingdom and start focusing on God and His love, as well as loving others. As we do this, the kingdoms of darkness will naturally fall and God will be exalted.

We need to recognize that whatever we focus on, we will empower, and my Bible says that satan is already defeated and under our feet (see Rom. 16:20). So what do we need to focus on him for?

If you will just begin to live a lifestyle of loving God and loving people, you will have victory in all of your battles with the enemy. Like I said earlier, I used to love to yell at demons in my meetings and cast them out for all to see, but now I don't even focus on them anymore. To be honest with you, if a demon manifests in a meeting nowadays, I will just let the ushers take the person manifesting the demon out of the meeting and let someone else deal with him or her.

I never focus on the devil anymore, and I will only deal with the demonic if I have to, but at the same time, I am not afraid of devils either. That's because I know that if a devil is manifesting in front of me, it is the devil who is really afraid of me, and it's that devil's last attempt to try to shake me of my confidence in the authority that God has given me because that devil already knows that he is defeated. Oftentimes the devil will come out of people immediately when I pray because I'm not empowering the demonic by focusing on them; I am focusing on the love of my Father who will set the person free.

CHAMPIONS OF LOVE

God wants us to shine for His glory and reveal the goodness and love of who He is to people everywhere we go. The requirement is intimacy with God. He wants to set us on fire so there will be tangible evidence that He is with us. When we are carrying the fire of the Holy Spirit on our lives, the reality of the goodness of God's love and glory will be seen upon us.

Zechariah 2:5 says, *"For I,' declares the LORD, 'Will be a wall of fire around her, and I will be the glory in her midst."* (NASB). God wants His people to embrace the torch of His love so we will be set on fire to show forth the reality of God's glory and love to those around us who don't know him. Are we willing to spend time with Jesus the Burning One until He sets us on fire for the world to see? Now is the time to get hungry for the goodness of God's love and glory to be seen in and through our lives. So let's spend time with Him, embracing the torch of His love and presence until we are set ablaze for Him and become carriers of His goodness and love.

BURNING ONES
BURN WITH THE SAME HEART AS JESUS

Everywhere Jesus went, He revealed His Father's love and goodness through signs, wonders, and miracles. He carried an anointing of the glory of God—an anointing of the Holy Spirit and power. He went about doing good and setting free all who were oppressed of the devil, for God was with Him (see Acts 10:38). This Scripture is a blueprint for us to see the purpose of the anointing of the Holy Spirit, both in the life of Jesus as well as ours. God wants to give us a new level of authority and power so that as Burning Ones, we can show people the Father's love.

In order to do so, God wants us to carry the right heart and mindset when it comes to His power and authority so that we can walk in a greater realm of power and authority than we have ever seen before. In John 14:12, Jesus said that we would do the same things as well as greater works than He did, but in order to do so, we must understand the heart of God about the miraculous. When Jesus was anointed with power, the purpose of that power was to do good.

God wants His Burning Ones to burn with the same heart as Jesus—a heart that longs to reveal the goodness and love of God the Father to a dying and lost world and to do good with the power He gives us.

We are living in a show-me generation among people who think that talk is cheap. They want to see something. They want a tangible evidence of the fact that God is who He really says He is in His Word, and God is raising up Burning Ones who are going to give people a taste of His goodness and love by releasing His power and glory everywhere they go.

What made Jesus different than all of the religious leaders of His day was that He didn't just talk about God, but He went about doing good, setting all oppressed by the devil free. Everywhere He went, He demonstrated God's love to people by casting out demons and healing all kinds of sickness and disease. As a result, people flocked to Him because they knew that God was really with Him. I believe that the Church must grab a hold of this understanding in this season. If Jesus went about doing good, demonstrating the goodness of who His Father was by releasing signs, wonders, and miracles to the people of His day, then we better get a hold of this understanding and begin to do the same in our day.

People in the world are looking for love, and it's up to us as the Church to reveal that love to them. One of the things I have been noticing as I have traveled all around the world is that people are tired of a powerless Christianity that communicates a message of legalism focused on sin. What people are hungry for is love—love that is tangible and able to be seen. God is raising up Burning Ones with a new mindset who are going to carry His love and demonstrate it to everyone everywhere they go. By releasing a genuine expression of power in love, transformation happens, and people leave their sinful lifestyles because they have seen something better and find what they are looking for—God's pure, real love.

God wants all that we do to be motivated by love, and when we are motivated by love, we will be willing to stop for the one unlovely person in our path and minister without being seen. And maybe that one person will be the key that unlocks the door to revival in a city or a nation.

BURNING ONES
RECOGNIZE THE SIGNIFICANCE OF ONE

Jesus had a heart for the unlovely, and He had a vision that was bigger than just preaching and teaching in the churches and synagogues of His day. He had a heart that burned for the lost and continually looked for opportunities to reach those who did not know Him or even realize that it was He they were longing for. For Jesus, it wasn't about the religious thinking of his day—that drawing a crowd was key to being rich and famous. He was all about seeing a harvest of souls come to know the Father in Heaven, and He did whatever it took to reach people—even if it didn't fit the packaged and canned traditions and religion of His day.

In John 4, we discover the heart and mandate of a Burning One and what it was that truly made Jesus a champion. It is here that we see what it was that motivated Jesus to do what He did when He walked the earth in the flesh. John 4:5-42 tells us the story of the Samaritan woman at the well. Jesus breaks out of the religious box of His day to stop to talk with one woman, a Samaritan woman, and stokes a fire of revival that causes salvation to come to a whole city. This story is an example of how the contagious fire of God's love can touch a person's life and break open a city so that an outpouring of God's love can be released.

One mark of the Burning Ones will be that they will walk as true revivalists who will have an ability to set others on fire and will carry an anointing to break open the hardest of atmospheres in order to see outpourings of God's Spirit happen that will affect entire cities, regions, and nations. So let's look at this story and find the heart of a Burning One.

> *So He came to a city of Samaria which is called Sychar, near the plot of ground that Jacob gave to his son Joseph. Now Jacob's well was there. Jesus therefore, being wearied from His journey, sat thus by the well. It was about the sixth hour. A woman of Samaria came to draw water. Jesus said to her, "Give Me a drink." For His disciples had gone away into the city to buy food.*

Then the woman of Samaria said to Him, "How is it that You, being a Jew, ask a drink from me, a Samaritan woman?" For Jews have no dealings with Samaritans.

Jesus answered and said to her, "If you knew the gift of God, and who it is who says to you, Give Me a drink, you would have asked Him, and He would have given you <u>living water</u>."

The woman said to Him, "Sir, You have nothing to draw with, and the well is deep. Where then do You get that living water? Are You greater than our father Jacob, who gave us the well, and drank from it himself, as well as his sons and his livestock?"

Jesus answered and said to her, "Whoever drinks of this water will thirst again, but <u>whoever drinks of the water that I shall give him will</u> never thirst. But the water that I shall give him will become in him a fountain of water springing up into everlasting life."

The woman said to Him, "Sir, give me this water, that I may not thirst, nor come here to draw."

Jesus said to her, "Go, call your husband, and come here."

The woman answered and said, "I have no husband."

Jesus said to her, "You have well said, 'I have no husband, for you have had five husbands, and the one whom you now have is not your husband; in that you spoke truly."

The woman said to Him, "Sir, I perceive that You are a prophet. Our fathers worshiped on this mountain, and you Jews say that in Jerusalem is the place where one ought to worship."

Jesus said to her, "Woman, believe Me, the hour is coming when you will neither on this mountain, nor in Jerusalem, worship the Father. You worship what you do not know; we know what we worship, for salvation is of the Jews. But the hour is coming, and now is, when the true worshipers will worship the Father in spirit and truth; for the Father is seeking such to worship Him. God is Spirit, and those who worship Him must worship in spirit and truth."

The woman said to Him, "I know that Messiah is coming (who is called Christ). When He comes, He will tell us all things."

Jesus said to her, "I who speak to you am He." And at this point His disciples came, and they marveled that He talked with a woman; yet no one said, "What do You seek?" or, "Why are You talking with her?" (John 4:5-27)

In this portion of Scripture, Jesus is doing the unthinkable. In His time and day, it was considered unlawful for a Jew to have contact or conversation with the Samaritan people, but Jesus was not moved by the traditions of people or religion. He was moved by the mandate and heart of His Father who was in Heaven. While everyone else in Jesus' time thought that the Jews were the only ones who would inherit salvation, God the Father had a different plan. His heart was not just to save the Jews, but all humankind. Jesus tapped right into that plan and stopped for the one.

John 3:16-17 gives us a glimpse of this great love the Father had for not just the Jews, but the entire world:

> For God so loved the world that He gave His only begotten Son, that whoever believes in Him should not perish but have everlasting life. For God did not send His Son into the world to condemn the world, but that the world through Him might be saved.

Most of the Jews of Jesus' day missed His coming because they did not recognize Him when He came. This was because when He came, He did not look the way they thought He would look. He came bringing a whole new understanding of things than what was expected of Him. The Jews thought He was coming to restore power back to the Jewish empire as a mighty king in the natural, but Jesus came with a mandate and plan that was much bigger. He came with a plan to save the whole world and become their King for all of eternity. He came to save all of humankind and not just one nation or one tribe.

Jesus came as a Burning One to reveal the love of His Father to the entire world and to restore relationship with God to all of humankind. From the very beginning of this encounter with this woman at the well, Jesus begins to break this religious box of the way people were taught in His time and day by simply asking this woman of Samaria for a drink of water. I believe Jesus knew very well what He was doing that day and that it was an important lesson for His disciples to learn about the heart of God toward others in the world beyond themselves.

What Jesus was communicating to this woman and His followers that day was that God is love, and He wants a relationship with whoever would receive His Son. In this story, you see Jesus ministering the fire of God to this woman as He reveals the secrets of her heart about her five husbands and she gets touched by the contagious fire of God. Her heart begins to open up to see Jesus in a different light.

At first, all she wanted to do was argue with Jesus about the tradition and religion of her day, but once she experienced the fire of God's love burning through Jesus' eyes and radiating from His presence, she realized that it was for her as well as the Jew. She caught fire.

And as she began to burn, a transformation happened in her heart, and the religious scales fell off of her eyes. She began to recognize that Jesus truly was the Christ sent from God to save the world. Completely set on fire by a revelation of God's love, she ran back to her city and spread the news about Jesus being the Christ, saying, *"Come, see a Man who told me all things that I ever did. Could this be the Christ?"* (John 4:29).

The Samaritans responded to her testimony and urged Jesus and His disciples to stay some extra days because they were hungry to encounter the same flame of love that so transformed and awakened the heart of the Samaritan woman at the well. An awakening started, and it began to spark an outpouring of God's Spirit in this city, and many people came to know Jesus as their Lord and Savior.

> *And many of the Samaritans of that city believed in Him because of the word of the woman who testified, "He told me all that I ever did." So when the Samaritans had come to Him, they urged Him to stay with them; and He stayed there two days. And many more believed because of His own word. Then they said to the woman, "Now we believe, not because of what you said, for we ourselves have heard Him and we know that this is indeed the Christ, the Savior of the world"* (John 4:39-42).

As the fire of God's Spirit began to awaken love in this city and the rains of God's Spirit began to fall, Jesus' disciples suddenly learned more about the heart of God regarding His love for people. They were confronted with the reality that God is love, and it looked different than what religion told them love would look like. They had to change the way they thought about Jesus and God's love and open up to the fact that God so loved the world and not just them—unbelievers, those who were considered unclean, unlovable, despised, and rejected individuals, those from other religions and cultures. It is so easy sometimes to just get caught up with the church world and that's it. Jesus had a heart for those in the Church as well as those in the world who didn't know God.

God wants to bring definition to what the mandate of a Burning One or a dread champion looks like. Who gets the power? Who is it for? Also, He wants to impart to us the same fire and zeal that Jesus burned with for the lost as when He was on the earth.

BURNING ONES
HAVE A "NOW" MINDSET

Now let's look at what Jesus told His disciples as they walked onto the scene of revival beginning to break out in the city of Samaria. Look at Jesus' response to them as they questioned in their hearts what He was doing and tried to get Him to eat something.

> Then they [the people of Samaria] went out of the city and came to Him [Jesus]. In the meantime His disciples urged Him, saying, "Rabbi, eat."
>
> But He said to them, "I have food to eat of which you do not know."
>
> Therefore the disciples said to one another, "Has anyone brought Him anything to eat?"
>
> Jesus said to them, "My food is to do the will of Him who sent Me, and to finish His work. Do you not say, 'There are still four months and then comes the

harvest?' Behold, I say to you, <u>lift up your eyes and</u>
<u>look at the fields, for they are already white for harvest!</u>
And he who reaps receives wages, and gathers fruit for
eternal life, that both he who sows and he who reaps
may rejoice together. For in this the saying is true: 'One
sows and another reaps.' <u>I sent you to reap</u> that for
which you have not labored; others have labored, and
you have entered into their labors" (John 4:30-38).

Now let's take look at this portion of Scripture and try to
bring some language to what Jesus is saying here. As Jesus begins
to talk to His disciples, He begins to teach them about what is
happening in the Spirit in the city of Samaria using the meta-
phor of food to teach them about what was happening right in
front of them.

What I believe Jesus was trying to do was to get His followers to take their eyes off of the natural and look at the supernatural. In this moment of time, <u>they were more worried about</u>
<u>eating food than embracing an outpouring of God's Spirit</u> that
was taking place right in front of their faces. Sometimes, when
God begins to move and release revival, people will miss it. The
reason is because when revival comes, it <u>often looks nothing like</u>
<u>what we think it's going to look like</u>. Sometimes God will offend
<u>you and show up in a way that you don't expect in order to test</u>
<u>your heart.</u>

<u>Jesus' disciples were probably thinking to themselves,</u> *This*
can't be a move of God. These people are Samaritans. They're not

the chosen people of God; we are. So many times God will pour out His Spirit on those who are not even looking for it.

God is looking for the hungry, not the qualified. Jesus goes on to talk about fields already white for harvest. I don't believe He was prophesying to them about the future. I believe He was saying to them, "Open your eyes; revival is happening right now in front of you."

Don't miss it. So many people have a mindset that God will move one day. Today is "one day." Jesus was burning to see the will of His Father come to pass and to partner with God to fulfill His work in the earth. He had a *now* Gospel of faith, a *now* mindset.

God wants to sound a clear trumpet blast of what we are called to do in the earth regarding His Kingdom as well as reveal to us our purpose and destiny here on the earth. I believe that through this story, God wants to give us language to the way we are to think and move as Burning Ones now in these end times. God wants us to stop waiting for Him to move in church and recognize that the harvest fields outside of the church are already ripe for the picking. God wants to anoint us with signs, wonders, miracles, and prophecies to bring in the harvest. And just like Jesus did, He wants us to see outpourings of God's Spirit overtake entire cities and regions and nations. God is *now* raising up Burning Ones who will carry an anointing of the supernatural to awaken the hearts of men and women to the love of the Father, and the result will be that outpourings of God's love will be seen wherever they go.

In the passage of Scripture about the woman at the well, we can see what Jesus' heart was burning for.

He came into the earth to gather souls, and He tells His followers not to waste any more time waiting for a harvest from God, but to believe for it *now*. He was encouraging them to gather souls—the fruit of the harvest. Jesus was trying to get the disciples' attention and cause them to discern the more important things of the Kingdom that were going on around them. He was trying to break the religious mold of the day, the thinking that far off in the future, when people go to Heaven, they will receive the miracles they need or see the promises of God fulfilled. He was showing them the value of things from a heavenly perspective. Jesus said, *"He who reaps receives wages, and gathers fruit for eternal life…"* (John 4:36). God is looking for those who will burn for souls, reap heavenly wages, and gather fruit for eternal life by winning souls into the Kingdom.

He also was communicating that the time was *now* and that they were stepping into a momentum fueled by the labors of those who had gone on before them, of those who had not yet seen the promises of God come to pass in their generation. He reveled that we need to partner with them in order to see their mandates fulfilled. Everywhere Jesus went, He was burning for God and preaching a *now* Gospel—a Gospel of Heaven invading earth today. God is releasing a momentum to us in our day that will cause us to reap the rewards for prayers we did not pray and breakthroughs for that which we did not work for in order to see His Kingdom manifest on earth and bring in an end-time harvest of souls.

BURNING ONES THINK STEPPING OUT OF RELIGIOUS ENCLAVES IS OK

God is raising up Burning Ones who will carry an anointing of revival fire to awaken the hearts of a generation to the love of their Father, and as a result, outpourings of God's Spirit will begin to be seen wherever they go, just like in the story of Jesus and the woman at the well. His encounter with this one woman unlocked a mighty outpouring of God to be seen in the city of Samaria. God wants to touch the hearts of people with His Spirit and cause them to become hungry for Him so He can pour out His Spirit upon them.

Do you get it? God wants to release outpourings of His Spirit—to you and through you. Acts 2:17-18 says:

> *And it shall come to pass in the last days, says God, that I will pour out of My spirit on all flesh; your sons and your daughters shall prophesy. Your young men shall see visions, your old men shall dream dreams And on My menservants and on My maidservants I will pour out My Spirit in those days; and they shall prophesy.*

The key for this to happen is for God's people to become carriers of God's fire. To walk as Burning Ones, demonstrating the love of the Father through signs, wonders, and miracles, unlocking the hearts of men to receive the rains of revival, we have to step out of our religious mindsets and cozy enclaves. We're not called to run off like a bizarre, zealous idiot, but to be intentional about listening to Jesus, drawing close to the flame of His love, and going where He sends us, some days stopping for the one and other days, releasing revival to a city.

Just like Jesus' disciples learned on that day in Samaria that God so loved the world—not just them—God wants us to begin to get a bigger vision. It is not just about what He is doing in our personal lives and at our churches. God wants us to get out from within the four walls of the church and to begin to partner with Him to pour out His Spirit on all flesh.

Burning Questions

Have you been turned off by religion or those who have been so weird in their expression of ministry that you want nothing to do with it? Perhaps past experiences led you to think that you were called to be an idiot revivalist and you ran the other way. You are called to become a Burning One—not an idiot. Are you ready to embrace the burning love of the Holy Spirit and enter into the deeper reality of the Kingdom of God and let His love and power flow through you?

Your Response

_____

_____

_____

_____

_____

_____

_____

_____

_____

_____

_____

_____

_____

_____

_____

_____

_____

A Prayer to Get You There

Lord, forgive me of the way I have perceived people, religion, and even You. Open my eyes to see You. Open my ears to hear You once again. I let go of my preconceived thoughts and fears and ask that You would set me up to encounter You, once again. I am Yours, every part of me. I surrender all to You and You alone. No more living for myself. I choose life. I choose You, just the way You have chosen me.

CHAPTER 2

LEAVE YOUR CAVE

God can take anyone and make him or her a champion overnight.

I was in the United Kingdom (UK) conducting some revival meetings in Dudley, England, ministering in the middle of what was called the Dudley Outpouring. Night after night, God was showing up in His goodness and love, healing and saving people. This revival lasted over 120 straight nights. One night while I was ministering on the platform, the Lord spoke to me, giving me several words of knowledge concerning different miracles He wanted to release that night. One of the words of knowledge He told me to speak out concerned someone in the meeting who was suffering from a severe stutter. He told me that this person had a speech impediment and He wanted to touch and heal this person. The Lord told me to announce to the people the condition as well as tell the crowd that God was going to heal this person on the spot. So I gave the word and said to the crowd, "If this is you, come up here now." A young man who was 21 years old came to the front and said that he was there to respond to this word of knowledge.

As I began to talk with him, it became very evident to everyone in the room that this young man had a problem with his speech. In fact, he could not speak out a sentence without stumbling over his words and stuttering. I heard the Holy Spirit tell me to touch his tongue and pray and he would be healed. I did just as the Holy Spirit instructed me to do, and instantly the young man's speech was healed. All of a sudden, he went from not being able to get words out of his mouth clearly without stuttering to screaming out the praises of God. As he began to cry out, people began to shout and praise God—including me.

Then after everyone calmed down, I began to interview the young man, and it became very evident to all who were in the room that God had done a mighty miracle. The young man went on to tell us that he had stuttered his whole life; as long as he could remember, he had had this problem. Then right before the young man sat down, I began to prophesy over him. I began by the Spirit of the Lord to tell this young man in front of 400 people in this meeting that God was going to raise him up to be a mighty healing revivalist and that God would use him and his testimony to touch the lives of many. I also told him that what had been a weakness in his life would now become a strength in his life. Then I went on to tell him that his mouth would now become a mouthpiece for God to preach His Word with signs, wonders, and miracles following. Then the man sat down and the meeting continued.

After the meeting was over, there were many gathered in the church coffee shop in the back of the church chatting. As this was going on, a man walked up to this young man and made a critical remark. He asked the young man whom God had healed if he really got touched by God and if he was really healed. When this young man heard this, he was filled with boldness and zeal and jumped up onto one of the tables in the coffee shop. Then he began screaming at the top of his lungs over the big crowd that had gathered in the coffee shop, "I want everyone to listen up."

As he did this, everyone became silent to hear what the young man had to say. Then he said, "Ever since I was a little boy, I have stuttered, and this man has the nerve to ask me tonight if God really healed me. I want everyone in this place to hear me right now. None of you have any idea what I have gone through. My whole life I have been known as a babbling idiot. I have been made fun of all of my life because I could not talk straight, and I want everyone in this place, including this man, to know that tonight Jesus Christ has healed me."

Those in the coffee shop broke out in praise to God, and people began to cheer. As this was happening, the man who had made this remark ran out of the coffee shop as quick as he could and was never seen again. A pastor who was in the coffee shop that night walked up to this young man and asked him if he would come speak at his church that Sunday and give a testimony of what God had done for him that night. The young man went to the pastor's church that next Sunday and shared his testimony and story. As he did, revival broke out. People started getting healed, saved, and delivered all over the place, and overnight, God birthed this young man into the ministry. Since that time, this young man has had many opportunities to preach and teach in many different churches and fellowships in England.

This young man's life and story is an example of what God is about to do in this hour. He is about to take the ones no one would believe could do anything for God and make them mighty champions for His name's sake. God called this young man out of his cave and into the spotlight to shine like a jewel in His hand for all to see. This young man went from the cave of isolation and insecurity to a place of faith and boldness overnight. One touch from the goodness of God can change everything. This young man received a touch of the justice of God that night and was launched overnight into his destiny and calling. He was the last person anyone from his community would have thought would go on to do great things for God—especially in the area of a vocational ministry. The other awesome thing was that not only did God do an awesome miracle in this young man's life, but He also immediately confirmed the prophetic word that I spoke over him that night.

BECOMING CHAMPIONS OF GOD

God wants to release an encounter to you that is so strong, so personal, that it will catapult you out of your cave and into your destiny as a champion of God.

God wants to release a supernatural acceleration. You know, there's a generation that's arising who just want Jesus; they don't want religion. They're not going to take ten years to get to a place of maturity and anointing. After four years of being saved, I started to travel all around the world. In the past four years, my wife and I have been in 28 different nations; we've seen hundreds of thousands of souls won for the Lord, and we've seen the Kingdom of God released in dark places.

God is about to take you from the cave to the spotlight. I believe that God is positioning many people to come out of a place of hiddenness and onto a platform. Position yourself to experience an encounter with God like you've never known before. Position yourself to receive more from God than you've ever dreamed. There is a lot going on in our personal caves. Some have hidden themselves because of hurt and disappointment, others because of pain or shame. Just one encounter with God will release justice to you, breaking the entrapment of the enemy off your life so you can emerge full of light and glory, ready to change the world.

From the Cave to the Company of Dread Champions

Now let's take a look at the life of David and his mighty men. David raised these men up and poured his life into them, and they became mighty champions for God. They were not anyone or anything special by any means. In fact, no one in that time and day would have expected any of the men David raised up to amount to anything. This was because all of the men whom David raised up were the rejects of Saul's kingdom. They were those who were known to be in debt, distressed, discouraged, and discontented with life. They were men who had run away from Saul and his kingdom to the caves of Adullam to be with David, who himself had run away from King Saul. The number of men who came to David in Adullam was around 400. (See First Samuel 22:1-2.)

David, a Burning One for God, took these distressed men and turned them into a mighty army of soldiers who would go on to win many battles for the Lord. David raise up mighty men of valor who, for the purposes of this book, are a picture of what dread champions look like.

As I began to study this, I found that even the place where David and his army met was significant. The Bible says that they met and were raised up at the Cave of Adullam. I looked up the meaning of this word *Adullam*, and it means *justice of the people*.[1] So God raised David and his mighty men up at the caves of justice. This, I believe, is a picture of what God is about to do in our time and day.

God is about to use the foolish things of the world to confound the wise, and He is going to make mighty champions out of people no one would have ever believed would do great things in their lives for God. Now is the time when God is going to begin to use the weak and foolish things of this world to demonstrate His greatness and love. It's a time when God is going to do the same in our day as He did with David and his mighty army. He is going to call people out of their caves and into action. He is going to cause His people to turn from running away from their enemies to defeating their enemies.

Many in the Church today feel like they are all alone and want to run away and hide in a cave rather than fight. They have spent much time pressing into God and paying the price of intimacy with Him, but have not seen results in their dreams and promises from God being fulfilled. As a result, they may be living in a place of hope deferred that makes the heart sick, feeling distressed, discouraged, and discontented with life or even the Church. For some, hopes have been so deferred that they have given up on the promises of God and settled into a cave of discouragement and hiddenness for a long time. Now is the time for the people of God to come out of the caves they have been hiding in and begin to fulfill the destinies and callings that God has promised them.

God is calling you out. It is time for justice to be released to you first. And what He does to you He'll do through you. He is calling you out of your cave of promiscuity and into a place of promotion with Him. He is calling you out of your cave of disappointment to begin to fulfill your destiny. He is calling you out of your cave of discontent and into the promises of God being fulfilled. He is calling you out of the cave of isolation and insecurity to a place of faith and boldness. He is calling you out of your cave and into the spotlight.

In David's army, not many were noble or powerful by any of the standards of his day, but God raised up an army that was victorious over the enemy and did great things for him anyway. Those who were in debt, distressed, discouraged, and discontented with life, He caused to become mighty champions for His name's sake.

I believe we are living in a day when God the Father is about to raise up a generation of dread champions though the principles of justice. And He will release to them seven-fold justice for the attacks of the enemy against their lives. I will cover much more on this subject of an army raised up by the principles of God's justice in some of the other chapters to come in this book. For now, let's look at who is emerging to answer the call.

Look Who's Coming Out of the Cave

Get ready for the hidden ones to come forth. Those God has been setting on fire in the secret place of His presence will emerge in the days to come carrying the fire of God in their bones and preaching the words of the Kingdom with faith, power, and substance.

Now is a time of promotion for those who have been in a place of faithfulness. God is calling people out of a season of hiddenness and into the light. Some of you have been in the cave of servanthood, learning to hear the voice of God and working on character by serving others and for others. This has felt more like a cave filled with discouragement and warfare than equipping for promotion.

God is about to make a distinction between the ones who love Him and the ones who don't, as well as the ones who are truly serving Him and His Kingdom with a pure heart and motive and those who don't. There are a lot of people in the Church who have been serving half their lives and feel like they have not stepped into their God-given destinies. Their hope has been deferred, and they wonder if anything they ever dreamed will come to pass. For those who feel like no one recognizes your anointing and gifting—now is your time to come out of a place of hiddenness! God has been working in you a heart to serve, and He has been birthing humility into a place of action.

I believe we are going to see some of the most amazing leaders the Body of Christ has seen emerge in this hour. They are those who have been faithful to serve and learn from the fathers and mothers God put in their lives. As a generation of champions begins to leave earth for the next step into eternity, God will begin to raise up a new generation of Burning Ones. Just as generals like Oral Roberts and Kenneth Hagin have passed on to be in glory with the Lord, I believe that God is looking for new generals to step into their shoes and take things even higher than they did. The key to stepping into that place is servitude and humility. Some people serve to get, but God is about to exalt those who have been serving with pure hearts. The reason it has taken so long for some is because God has been crushing and burning every hindrance out of their lives so they can truly stand in a greater level of glory than those who have gone on before us.

For some, you have been in a season like Elijah was in First Kings 19 when he ran away from the people of God and hid himself away in a cave on the mountain of God due to the warfare that was coming against his life after his great victory on Mount Carmel.

He had just seen the power of God working through him to turn the heart of his nation away from the enemy and back to God, and instead of remaining in a place of victory, he ran from Jezebel and forgot about the mighty victory he had just had. Then God came to him in the cave and began to call him back out and tell him that there was still work that God had for him to do. God told him to stop his whining and go anoint Jehu as king of Israel, as well as anoint Elisha as a prophet to replace him.

Some of the greatest fathers and mothers are going to emerge in this hour to raise up champions who will be Burning Ones who will change the world. A lot of these fathers and mothers are ones who have seen God move mightily in the past and experienced the things of the Kingdom, but somewhere along the journey in life, they allowed the religious spirit to hinder them, toss them in the cave of isolation, and bury their talents.

God is calling the Body of Christ out of a place of defeat and into a place of action. This next move of God is not just going to be a move of God where God is going to use the young ones, but will be a move where God is going to merge the generations.

It will be a move of fathers, mothers, sons, and daughters. In order for this move to happen, the older generation must begin to step back up to the plate and begin to listen to the voice of God's Spirit. He is calling the older ones who have been living in a place of isolation and defeat back into action. It is time for the wounded in Christ to be healed, to take their place as generals in the army of God, and to see a generation of Burning Ones emerge.

Elijah did not stay in the cave of sorrows and defeat. He left the cave and called forth that which was not as if it was, and Jezebel was eventually defeated by the spiritual children God gave Elijah in Jehu and Elisha. God wants to raise up a generation of sons and daughters, but needs the fathers and mothers to take their place once again.

God wants to release revival fire to those who have been in a place of hurt, pain, and sorrows and cause them to burn again. He also wants to release more fire to those who are already burning so they will burn even brighter in the days to come.

In fact, God has been speaking to me about the next move of revival. He has been telling me, "Jerame, don't look to a certain church or geographical location or region for revival to happen. The next revival I send is going to take place in the hearts and minds of My people, and I am going to cause them to become carriers of revival. They will begin to carry a spirit of revival that will result in revival happening everywhere they go."

You might ask the question, "What is revival?" True revival is when someone has an encounter with God's Spirit and is never the same again. It's like the day you gave your life to Jesus. Something radical happened in your heart, and you went from one direction of living to another direction and never looked back. Revival is when God changes someone's heart and sets him or her on fire to want to know Him more.

God wants to give us burning bush experiences like Moses had in the Old Testament to change us and cause us to go from glory to glory and become witnesses of Him in the earth. He had an encounter with God's fire that resulted in all of his insecurities and fears being burned out of his life, an encounter that transformed him into a mighty champion or Burning One for God. God wants us to carry this spirit of revival everywhere we go, releasing it into the lives of those who don't know Him so that radical change can happen in their hearts and they would get saved.

God is about to raise up a new breed of champions for His glory, those who will carry the spirit of revival in everyday life. God does not want to be put in the box of only healing miracles and prophecy. He wants to change and affect every aspect of society. He is raising up Burning Ones in the business world, arts, entertainment, sports, and even political realms. It's time for the people of God to begin to dream big and grab a hold of the gift of influence. God wants to give His people influence to bring the lost into the Kingdom and justice to the land.

Look, people are emerging from their caves all around you. Come out! Leave the cave of discouragement, insecurity, fear, and disappointment and receive the justice of God.

Burning Ones Become Dread Champions Who Release Justice

As you emerge from the cave and receive the justice of God, you will soon find out that your purpose as a Burning One is to become a dread champion who boldly, empowered by the Holy Spirit, releases His justice to others. The devil has stolen much from our lives: our purpose and destiny, our health, finances, relationships, and dreams. He's stolen from many people, and God wants to release justice through you. What does justice look like?

I remember being in Seoul, Korea, preaching in this revival meeting on the justice of God, and we released a healing wave. All these people got healed, and it was awesome! People came up on the platform and started giving their testimonies, and all of them seemed to repeat a similar phrase, "Yes, this is the justice of God."

"So what did God do for you?" I asked the first woman.

She replied, "Well, I used to be a professional piano player. About five years ago, suddenly my hand became paralyzed for no reason. The doctors couldn't tell me why, and I can't explain what happened. All I know is that I could no longer move my hand for the past five years."

So after I heard her testimony I ask her, "So you're healed now?"

She said yes.

And I found myself replying, "That's the justice of God," as I continued to minister under the anointing of God. Then I went on to say, "You know what? On top of receiving your healing, God's going to give you a healing ministry. Go over there on that piano and play us some music." So she got on the piano and started playing. God's glory fell in the room, and many started getting healed all over the place.

Then, about a year later, I heard that this woman had been traveling all around Korea ministering on her keyboard, and people were getting saved and healed everywhere she went.

And then another boy, about 16 years old, came up, and I asked, "What did God do for you?"

He replied, "Man, this is justice. God just totally healed my eye."

And I said, "OK, cool, man, so what's the deal?"

Then he said to me, "Well, my whole life I have had a dream in my heart to be a fighter pilot. I've always wanted to fly planes. But the problem is they told me I never could because I've got a bad cataract in my left eye."

It was amazing. God had totally removed the cataract, instantly healing him. He was super happy as he ended his testimony by saying, "I'm gonna live my dream. I'm gonna live my dream."

God is going to begin to release the justice of God to the Body of Christ. He's going to begin to raise up those that have been stricken by the enemy, to release justice and take back what the enemy has stolen from others.

Then the next guy came forward, and I asked, "What happened to you?" He had another eye miracle.

"I was color blind my whole life, and I wanted to be a jeweler and was told that I couldn't do it because I couldn't see the color of the gems. Ever since I was little, I have had this passion in my heart to have my own jewelry business. Now I can do it! God has restored the color. I've never seen colors, and now I can see them."

It's amazing. The justice of God will release destiny. Dread champions release justice as they move in the love and power of the Holy Spirit. Are you ready to step into your destiny as a dread champion of God? Are you ready to help others reach theirs?

The Invitation Has Been Issued

Who were these "mighty men of David"? The Bible says of David's mighty men that they were fierce warriors who had faces like lions and feet like gazelle, were swift as gazelles, and were experts with the shield, spear, and bow (see 1 Chron. 12:8). They even could throw stones with both hands to destroy enemy soldiers, and they were amazing with the sword. The least of these men could slay hundreds of men at one time, and the mightiest of these warriors could slay a thousand enemy soldiers with one sword and not be touched. These men could also scale or leap over a wall and run down their enemies by the power of God (see Ps. 18:29). They formed a great army like the army of God (see 1 Chron. 12:22).

I believe that David and his mighty men are a metaphorical picture of what God is about to do in this hour. They are a picture of the anointing that will rest upon the dread champions or Burning Ones in the days to come. They will be a company of believers who will carry the might and kingship of God upon their lives and will destroy the works of darkness everywhere they go without fail. They will be those who are expert fighters with the tools and gifts that God has given them, and they will live to give glory to the King as well as strike fear into the enemy's camp.

History has a way of repeating itself. Just like in the days of David where wickedness was allowed unbridled expression and God raised up David and these mighty champions to demonstrate His authority and power, He is going to do it again in our time and day. And people will marvel at the lives of His champions and give glory to God. God is not going to raise up only the qualified; He is going to raise up the willing—those who are willing to pay the price for friendship with God and believe Him for big things despite the odds that may face them. One touch from the master can change everything. God is going to begin to use the ones who are least likely to shine for His glory and make them dread champions who bring glory and honor to His name.

I had a dream one night about a year before I wrote this book, and in this dream I was on a bus. I was driving somewhere on this bus, and next to me sat a spiritual father of mine named Bobby Connor. I pulled out an envelope that seemed like a wedding invitation. Then, I handed it to Bobby, and he opened it up, looked at it, and said, "Yup, that's the word of the Lord right there."

So I look over at the card that he was holding and noticed this phrase that was written on the card. It said, "Sons of Light." Then Bobby looked at me in my experience and started to prophesy, saying, "Jerame, you have traveled all around the world, and you have seen revival, as well as awesome miracles. But something greater is about to happen. The dread champions are about to step onto the scene."

After I came out of this dream, I began to pray to the Lord for the understanding of the dream, and the Lord began to speak to me. He said that the bus represented a move of the Spirit and that the next move of the Spirit would be that the sons of light, the dread champions, would emerge onto the scene, and that they would do great things for God's glory.

The dread champions are those who are like the mighty men of David.

He wants to set us apart. He wants to put an anointing on our lives that everywhere we go we destroy the works of darkness—just like Jesus did. He manifested Himself to destroy the works of darkness. And Jesus said, "You'll do the same things that

I do and greater works shall you do" (See John 14:12). Are you ready to do them?

He is calling us out of our caves and enclaves. Will you come?

BURNING QUESTIONS

What is your cave? Is it a cave of obscurity? Is it a cave of disappointment? Or is it a cave filled with electronic toys and games that keep you locked in a fantasy world that has nothing to do with really living and experiencing your destiny and fulfilling your purpose in life? Do you like to hide or are you hiding because of fear or shame? Did you know that God created you to live life abundantly—not cowering away in pain or shame? What will it take for you to come out of your cave?

Your Response

_____

_____

_____

_____

_____

_____

_____

_____

_____

_____

_____

_____

_____

_____

_____

_____

_____

_____

A Prayer to Get You There

Lord, I am ready to come out. I am willing to walk into my destiny as a Burning One, as one who is called to do great exploits for You and with You. Lead me out of my cave. I make a declaration, right now, that I am coming out from hiding. I renounce the cave, and I take Your hand in mine. Lead me out, lead me higher. I trust You, Lord. And I surrender myself to Your great plans and purposes for me. I will go where You lead me. Come and reveal, even this week, through the Word or through others, the first step. Where do You want me to go from here?

Endnote

1. *Blue Letter Bible,* s.v. "Adullam"; http://www.
blueletterbible.org/lang/lexicon%20/lexicon.
cfm?Strongs=H5725&t=NASB; accessed April 18, 2011.

CHAPTER 3

EMBRACE THE FIRE

Most everyone who finds themselves succeeding in work or in ministry today faced a decision to step out of their caves of personal fears and conflict—and they took that step only to discover that not far from the cave raged a firestorm ready to consume them. It takes a strong encounter with the Lord to cause us to leave our caves. We need that encounter not to boost our egos, but to strengthen us to walk through the fires of opposition that burn within us, in our minds, and without, by those who come against us.

One of the marks of the dread champions will be that they will be a generation who will embrace the fire of God, not run from it. They will be those who are willing to pay the price necessary to become carriers of His glory. They will not be consumed by the flames; they will become flames. They will become Burning Ones. They will be those who will burn for Jesus, and others will take note. John the Baptist was a Burning One. Jesus said of him that he was a bright and shining lamp and that people came to the light of his burning for God (see John 5:35). I believe that God wants us to burn brightly for Him everywhere we go and reveal His goodness and love to a dying and lost generation. Also, I believe that if we will embrace the fire of God, it will unlock the miraculous in our lives, and we will really walk as Jesus did when He was in the earth.

Even Jesus had to leave His cave—the cave of obscurity—and step into the public. He knew that the public would embrace Him one day and turn on Him the next. Yet He went. As soon as He stepped forth, He received the baptism, not just of water when His cousin John baptized Him in the Jordan, but of the Holy Spirit. When He received the baptism of the Holy Spirit, He did not just receive a baptism of the Holy Spirit, but He received a baptism of the Holy Spirit and fire. Immediately afterward, Jesus began to embrace the trials by fire, willingly stepping up to the test as satan met Him in the wilderness:

> Immediately the Spirit drove Him into the wilderness...forty days, tempted by Satan, and was with the wild beasts; and the angels ministered to Him (Mark 1:12-13).

Jesus moved out of His "cave" and into the "fire." However, the ordeal only made Him stronger. After He had paid the price of going though the fire and overcoming the temptations of the enemy, He came out of the wilderness in the power of the Spirit.

This is what happened after Jesus embraced the fire of God in His time in the wilderness.

Then Jesus returned in the power of the Spirit to Galilee and news of Him went out through all the surrounding region. And He taught in their synagogues, being glorified by all (Luke 4:14-15).

Jesus never did one miracle or preached one sermon until after He walked with God through the fire. After He embraced the fire of God, He stepped into His God-given destiny and calling and was given the right to access the supernatural power of God.

We must embrace the fire of God to obtain the precious things of God's anointing. So many people desire to have angelic visitations and encounters with God, but are not willing to pay the price to get them. It was after a time of embracing the fire in the wilderness that the angels of Heaven began to minister to Jesus as well. When we receive the baptism of the Holy Spirit and fire, it begins to open up the supernatural to us as well. After God began to teach me all of this, I began to realize that this was why the Bible says that *many are called, but few are chosen* (see Matt. 20:16). Not everyone who is a Christian is willing to pay the price necessary to become carriers of God's fire.

Jesus went through the fire and came out of the fire *on* fire. Everywhere He went from that point on, He was a bright and shining lamp for God, moving in signs, wonders, and miracles and releasing the flame of His Father's love to everyone He came into contact with. It was as He embraced the baptism of the Holy Spirit and fire that He then became a Burning One for God.

Every one of us is called to embrace the fire.

I remember one of the first times I walked with God through His fire. I was a young Christian, just emerging from my cave. I was so young that the episode I am about to tell you could have easily derailed me from my calling. It happened to me right after I had just discovered my authority in Christ as a young believer. I was fresh off of a missions trip to India and had been attending a more conservative church led by a young, 24-year-old pastor for a couple of years. At the time, I had just discovered that Jesus was a healer, for on that trip to India, I had seen, for the first time in my life, God move in miraculous ways. As we prayed for the sick in India, the blind began to see, the deaf heard, the crippled walked, and demons were cast out. It was an amazing time in my life, and I was so excited about the things that I was seeing God doing regarding the miraculous.

Once home from India, I wanted to just keep the momentum going. I kept praying for people who needed miracles and casting out demons when I met people who needed deliverance. I was seeing God do miracles everywhere I went—in the streets, malls, restaurants, and my work place. After about six months of praying for people everywhere I was going and seeing God touch and save people, I began to realize that not everyone in my church saw the Kingdom of God and the miraculous the way I saw it.

One night after a church service, one of the elders of the church came to me and asked me about all of the miracles I had been seeing. I excitingly began to tell him about so many of the testimonies of the healings and miracles I had been seeing in the streets. Then all of a sudden, he interrupted me and said, "I need to bring a warning to you, brother. I think you had better be careful with all of this healing stuff. I think, if you're not careful, it's going to get out of control and go sideways down the road." Then he went on to tell me that healing was not the best way to reach people.

Being a young Christian, I began to quote to him Scriptures about how healing was part of the Gospel. As I did, he got angry and started yelling at me in front of a couple hundred people and then ran out of the building. It was a weird and awkward moment for sure. He ran out, and I was left with all these people just staring at me. The following weekend, I woke up to get ready for Sunday church, and I received a phone call from one of the assistant pastors. He said that the pastor wanted to have a meeting with me after the service. I knew it most likely had to do with the argument I had gotten into a few nights before at the midweek meeting with the elder, so I told them that I would meet with him. When church ended that day, the pastor asked me to come meet with him in the park. Much to my surprise, there were about 10 people waiting at a picnic table for me—all of the elders of the church, deacons, and men from the church board. Then I noticed three of my friends who I had been hanging out with, ones I had been discipling and teaching, were there also.

We sat down and all these men began to accuse me of crazy rumors and things that I had never said. They started saying stuff like, "You have been telling people that unless they speak in tongues, they're not really saved," among other things. Then finally, one of the elders gave my friends and me an ultimatum, saying, "Here is the deal. All of this supernatural stuff isn't from God. You guys need to stop prophesying, praying for the sick, and casting out demons or you have to go."

At that point I had to speak up. "Hold on. All of you are saying crazy things that are not true. Can I have a moment to share my heart?"

They told me to go for it. So I opened my Bible to the Book of Ephesians and began to share with them about how some were called to be apostles, some prophets, some evangelists, and others pastors and teachers. As I did, I began to honor them and said to them, "You guys are amazing teachers of the Word and are amazing pastors, and I respect and honor you for that. But just because someone is different than you doesn't mean that you just get rid of them. The Bible says that we are all called differently, and we need each other, and just because I am moving in a prophetic and evangelistic calling doesn't make it wrong."

Then I went on to say, "We need each other. I need you, and you need me."

Then right when I said that, one of the elders screamed out, "That's the crap that Benny Hinn believes and it's off." Suddenly, everyone started yelling and arguing with me like crazy. As this happened, I realized the conversation was going nowhere and just got up, walked off, got in my car, and drove home.

I said to myself on my drive home, *Guess I'm not going back there anymore.*

THE FIRE OF HUMILITY
RELEASES AUTHORITY

But later that week, I had a dream, and in the dream I went back to the church and found the elder I originally got in an argument with and walked up to him and said, "Please forgive me for acting the way I did. Sorry for offending you. I was wrong."

Then the joy of the Lord hit us both, and I woke up.

When I first woke up from the dream, I was upset and said to myself, *There is no way I'm going back there and apologizing. I didn't even do anything wrong.*

Then God spoke to me more clearly than I had ever heard Him speak before: "Humble yourself and go back and apologize."

Then I said to God, "That's not fair. I didn't even do anything wrong."

He said, "I never asked you if you were right. Do what you are told."

So I went and humbled myself and showed up at the next midweek service, and to my surprise, the first person I ran into was this elder. He was shocked to see me, so I did just like in my dream, and I said I was sorry and asked for his forgiveness. As I did this, the joy of the Lord hit us both, and he said to me that he forgave me.

Then the pastor noticed that I was there and sent for me, so I went up front and sat down alone with him. He asked me if I had made my decision to stay or leave yet. I told him I felt like I was supposed to move on. Then he said to me that that was what he thought I would end up telling him. He went on to tell me that even though a lot of the people on his board and team didn't believe that the things happening in my life were really God, he did, and he encouraged me and said, "Don't stop going hard after God, and don't stop doing the things you are doing." He then went on to say to me that Paul and Barnabus had moments like this in the Bible, and both moved on to serve God mightily. He said, "I feel like this is one of those moments, and as your pastor, I bless you to move forward in your destiny and bless you to find a new church."

It was awesome what God did. Because I was obedient to humble myself and apologize to the elder, God turned something that could have been destructive and could have left me with a wound in my heart toward leaders, and He caused it to be a blessing. So many people have bad experiences early in their walks with God, but when you do what God says when He says to do it, you will walk through the fire of attack that the enemy sets before you to stop you, and you will emerge stronger than before, unburnt, with not a hair on your head singed.

God also told me afterward that because I humbled myself and repented to the elder, it opened the door for me to have authority to pray for that church in the Spirit. So I began to pray that the Holy Spirit would invade that place. About two years later, God prompted me to go back and visit a service at the church. Much to my surprise, my friend who was the pastor preached that day on how they needed to begin to pursue a relationship with the Holy Spirit and how God showed him that people needed to rely on the Holy Spirit more than on other people. It was the very thing I had been praying for to happen at this church since I had left. God is so good that He allowed me to be there to see that He had started to answer that prayer.

All kinds of amazing things can happen if we humble ourselves, and even though I wasn't in the wrong that day when I came before that counsel of men, God turned it around for good. Jesus wasn't wrong either on the day they crucified Him, but because He humbled Himself and forgave, He leaped over the walls of fire and death and purchased the victory that we are still living in today.

Living Flame of Love

Just recently I had a visitation where God began to speak to me about the importance of the fire of God in the lives of His people. I was in Austin, Texas, attending some tent revival meetings in a tent with a friend of mine—Rodney Howard Browne. As the worship was wrapping up for the night, I felt an intense presence of the Lord come over me, and I went into an open vision. In this vision, I saw an angel of the Lord appear on my right side. As I looked at him, I noticed that he was carrying a large torch of fire in his right hand. The appearance of it reminded me of the kind of torch that an Olympic athlete would carry or run around with at the beginning of the opening ceremonies of the Olympic games.

As I began to fix my eyes on this huge torch of fire that the angel was carrying, he reached out his hand and gave it to me. I could feel the weight of the torch in my hand as I grabbed a hold of it. I also noticed that there was a Scripture engraved upon the handle of it. The Scripture read, "Romans 8:11." As I noticed the Scripture, I could see and feel the intense heat of the flame of fire that was coming off of the torch. The flame of fire that was coming out of the torch was unlike any other flame I had ever seen. It was powerful, and yet at the same time, it had a life of its own. It was like the fire was alive as it burned, and there was an overwhelming sense of God's love and presence that seemed to radiate from the torch. It was like the flame of fire oozed the love of God. Then all of a sudden, as I was looking at this beautiful sight and feeling overwhelmed by God's great love, I noticed that the angel who had handed me the torch had disappeared and that there was a different angel now standing in front of me watching me as I handled the torch.

This angel was much different than the first one who had handed me the torch. This angel was dressed in a white robe and had a golden sash across his chest. He held a pad of paper in one hand and a pen for writing in his other. I could see that his eyes were fixed on me, but he was not looking at my face. In fact, he never made eye contact with me once. It seemed like all he did was stare right at my chest. I realized that he was staring right at my heart. And once I realized this, I began to feel a physical sensation of the gaze of his eyes burning into my heart. Within seconds, the vision ended.

As I came out of the encounter, I was shocked as well as excited. I knew that something very significant had just happened and that God was speaking to me about something very big. All I could do for about the first five minutes was think about the torch and the living flame of love that it contained, as well as the Scripture that was engraved on it. While I was meditating on these things, the Holy Spirit began to speak to me. One of the first things He told me was that now is the time when He is going to begin to raise up the Burning Ones. He explained, "The Burning Ones will be a generation, both young and old, who will carry the torch of My presence to the nation and reveal My love and power to people everywhere they go. If My people will embrace the fire of the Holy Spirit, then I will give to them the torch of My presence that the angel handed to you in your vision as well as the anointing of the Scripture that was written upon it. And they will begin to walk in resurrection life and power—just as Jesus did when He walked the earth."

Then He began to speak to me about the second angel in my vision. He said, "Jerame, remember the angel that appeared in front of you with a pen and pad of paper. He is a watcher angel sent from Heaven into the earth to watch over My word in order to perform it. Right now, all of Heaven is watching the hearts of men to see if they will embrace the fire of God."

When the Lord spoke this to me, I remembered how the angel would not look me in the eyes, but only stared at my heart.

Then the Lord said, "The angels of Heaven are now on assignment to watch the hearts of people, and to those they find who are willing to embrace the fire of God and pay the price for true intimacy with Him, they are to write their names down on the pad of paper and give the names to the Father in Heaven so He will know who to release His word over."

Then the last thing he told me was this: "You have been found faithful in spending time in My presence and have been chosen to carry the torch of My presence and love to the nations. Everywhere you go, you will see the real manifestation of the baptism of the Holy Spirit and fire as well as notable remarkable signs and wonders that will follow the preaching of this message. And you will call forth others who will be chosen to be Burning Ones as well."

After God spoke all of these things to me, the first thing I did was begin to look things up in the Word of God. After all, I believe that the visitations we have must line up with the Word of God or they are not really from Him. The first Scripture I looked up was Romans 8:11. I really wanted to know what this Scripture said since it was on the torch and the Lord told me that He was going to give this Scripture and anointing to those who were willing to embrace the fire of the Holy Spirit.

Romans 8:11 says:

> *But if the Spirit of Him who raised Jesus from the dead*
> *dwells in you, He who raised Christ from the dead will*
> *also give life to your mortal bodies through His Spirit*
> *who dwells in you.*

As I read this Scripture, I was amazed and excited at the same time. I realized that it perfectly lined up with the vision and what God was telling me. God was saying that if His people would embrace the fire of His Spirit, as well as pay the price of true intimacy with Him, He would entrust them with the ability to walk in resurrection life and power and cause them to walk just like Jesus did when He was in the earth. This Scripture was all about resurrection life and power, as well as how the same Spirit that raised Christ Jesus from the dead was alive and dwelling inside of us.

Just as I was thinking about this, the Lord began to speak to me again. He said to me, "Jerame, the Church has been crying out for more of My presence and more of My power, and I want to give it to them, but the key for them to begin to receive it will be for them to begin to embrace and understand the fire of God."

Then He went on to say, "There has been a lot of teaching and preaching on the subject of the Holy Spirit, and there are a lot of people who love the goosebumps, joy, and miracles that the Spirit of God brings, but not many in the Church today are teaching on the subject of the Holy Spirit and fire. It's my desire to begin to release to My people more revelation on the fire of the Holy Spirit, for it is the fire of My presence that will purify them to the place where they can walk in resurrection life and power, as well as cause them to become carriers of the flame of My love."

After I heard God say these things, I began to realize that He was right. I had heard a hundred messages on the Holy Spirit since I had been saved, especially when it came to the manifestations of God's Spirit and the gifts of the Spirit, but I had only heard a handful of messages on the fire of God. After I thought about this for a while, I began to ask God for more revelation regarding the Holy Spirit and fire.

Embrace the Fire of God

As I was thinking about all that He said to me, I began to think of the passage in Luke 3:16-17 where John the Baptist said he came to baptize people in water, but there would be one who was greater than him who would come baptizing with the Holy Spirit and fire. This passage reveals some interesting truths about the baptism of the Holy Ghost and fire that lined up with what God spoke to me about in my vision.

> John answered, saying to all, "I indeed baptize you with water; but One mightier than I is coming; whose sandal strap I am not worthy to loose. He will baptize you with the Holy Spirit and fire. His winnowing fan

is in His hand, and He will thoroughly clean out His threshing floor, and gather the wheat into His barn; but the chaff He will burn with unquenchable Fire" (Luke 3:16-17).

As I read this, I saw very clearly what God was talking about. In this portion of Scripture, you see John talking about how he baptized in water, but when Jesus would come, He would baptize with the Holy Spirit and fire. After reading this, I began to realize that most churches out there are baptizing people in water and preaching some on the Holy Spirit, but not many are embracing the fire of God's Spirit.

As I thought about this, I reflected on the latter half of John's prophecy about the baptism of fire that Jesus would bring. In the latter half, John begins to prophesy about what would happen when the fire of God would begin to be released through Jesus' baptism. He said, *"His winnowing fan is in His hand, and He will thoroughly clean out His threshing floor, and gather the wheat into His barn; but the chaff He will burn with unquenchable Fire"* (Luke 3:17).

In this parable, John used language from the time and day he lived in to teach the people some simple truths about what the baptism of the Holy Spirit and fire would look like. In John's day, the way they took up the harvest was different than the way we do it today with our combines and machinery. What they would do is this—after they pulled up the wheat by hand, they brought it to a barn where it would undergo a refining process. They would then take a winnowing fork that is similar to a pitchfork and use it to throw the newly cut wheat up in the air. This resulted in a separation of the chaff from the wheat. As they would throw the wheat up in the air, the chaff would fall upon the threshing floor and remain there until it would be burned up with fire. The wheat would be put in a barn to sell. The good would be separated from the bad in this process.

It is a picture of what the anointing of fire is supposed to do in our lives. When the Holy Spirit and fire come into our lives, it will separate that which is born of the flesh from that which is born of the Spirit of God, and it will destroy every stronghold that hinders us from seeing and knowing God.

OUCH

As I studied this out, I realized the reason why the fire of God was not the most popular message out there. It was because when the baptism of fire is released into someone's life, it comes to purge. It will purge or burn away everything in our lives that hinders us from knowing God more, as well as everything that hinders us from going deeper in our relationships with Him. One reason churches avoid the topic of the fire of God is because they would rather stay comfortable. Another reason is that most don't understand what the fire is.

So many people, when they talk about the fire of God, act as if it is a bad thing or as if they are going through hell as they embrace it. The truth of the matter is that the fire of God won't kill you, but it will help you to become more like Jesus. The fire that God wants us to embrace is not the fire of His judgment. The fire of His judgment is to be saved up for the final Day of Judgment when God will judge satan and all of his evil hordes, along with all of those who reject Jesus as Lord and Savior. The fire that God wants us to embrace now is the transforming power of His love.

When I handled the torch the angel gave me in my vision, the one thing I noticed was that the flame that was coming off of it was pure love. It was the most amazing feeling of God's love that was radiating off of it. It was not a scary or condemning feeling that came off of the fire. It was an intense feeling of the love of God.

One of the things we need to understand about God's fire is that it is His love.

Song of Solomon 8:6-7 reads:

> *Set me as a seal upon your heart, as a seal upon your arm; for love is as strong as death, jealousy as cruel as the grave, its flames are flames of fire, a most vehement flame. Many waters cannot quench love, nor can the floods drown it. If a man would give for love all the wealth of his house, it would be utterly despised.*

In this Scripture, we see an example of God's fiery love. God's love is intense toward us. This Scripture tells us that nothing can quench God's love, not even death itself or even many waters or the mightiest of floods. God loves us too much to allow us to stay the same.

The Bible tells us that there is no greater love than that demonstrated by people who would lay down their lives for their friends (see John 15:13). Jesus came in the flesh to demonstrate the fiery love of God to humankind. John 3:16 says,

> For God so loved the world that he gave His only begotten Son, that whoever believes in Him should not perish but have everlasting life.

The reason Jesus came from Heaven to earth to become a man and die on the cross was because God loved the world. Because of the fall of Adam, we are all born into a fallen state of mind and being, but Jesus came in the likeness of humanity to burn with the love of our Father and set us free from the law of sin and death. He came to make a way for us to be in right standing with the Father again.

Adam lost the right to live and move in the glory of God because of his sin, but Jesus came to redeem us from this curse and give us access again to the precious presence of God's glory though the power of His blood and the forgiveness of our sins. God loves us too much to allow us to stay the same. The fire of God is His love, and as we spend time with God getting to know Him and his Word, our lives are changed.

We need to understand that all whom God loves He chastens. In Revelation 3:14-22, Jesus challenges the lukewarm church of the Laodiceans. He confronts them and tells them to come out of a place of being lukewarm in their hearts toward God and to become either hot or cold for Him. Then He goes on to tell them that though they think they are rich and have need of nothing, they are really wretched, miserable, poor, blind, and naked. Then He says to the church of Laodicea,

> *I counsel you to buy from Me gold refined in the fire, that you may be rich; and white garments, that you may be clothed, that the shame of your nakedness may not be revealed; and anoint your eyes with eye salve, that you may see* (Revelation 3:18).

This seems like a harsh word to bring to people, but then in the very next verse Jesus goes on to say, *"As many as I love I rebuke and chasten. Therefore be zealous and repent"* (Rev. 3:19). In this part of Scripture, we see Jesus talking to a bunch of people who think they have it all together. He ends up bringing a word of correction to the Laodicean church and then goes on to encouraging them to buy gold from Him that was refined by fire.

The result for those who were willing to remain hot for God and change their ways was that they would have access to the precious things of the Kingdom. There are several things in this parable that Jesus said would happen if this church would embrace the fire of God. As we walk with God through the fire, we will be given white garments and the shame of our nakedness will be covered. What this is talking about is that when we have gone through the refining process of the fire of God, we will come out of the process clean in spirit and walking in purity.

Also, this portion of Scriptures says that as we embrace God's fire, we will be anointed with eye salve in order to see in the Spirit. So many people want to see in the Spirit, but are unwilling to consecrate themselves and embrace the flame of God's love, so they never end up entering into the deeper things of God for themselves. It is the pure in heart who will see God (see Matt. 5:8). Jesus wants us as His people to buy from Him gold refined by fire. What He is really saying is, it's time for the Church to understand that they must pay the price for the precious things of the Kingdom of God, and that price is to embrace the fire of God.

When the fire of God comes, it will purge or bring to the surface all of the bad attitudes and intents in people's lives and remove them so that purity is all that remains. One of the things the Lord told me when He was giving me the interpretation of my vision was that it was His desire to begin to release more revelation on the fire of the Holy Spirit to His people, because it was the fire of His presence that would purify them to the place where they could walk in resurrection life and power, as well as cause them to become carriers of the flame of His love. There is a purifying process God wants us, as the children of God, to go through. It's not just about being baptized in water and confessing Jesus as your Lord and Savior or just being baptized in the Holy Spirit and moving in the gifts of God. It's about transformation. And if you want to be transformed, you need to go deeper with God. You need to be in His face and willing for Him to get in your face.

I was preaching on the fire of God during a meeting in Murfreesboro, Tennessee, when the fire of God began to fall in the meeting, and I saw God illustrate this point about how quickly He can transform someone who is willing to embrace the fire.

A young man who was attending the meetings was new to the things of the Spirit. He was the son of the host of the conference and had recently begun to really seek the Lord in a significant way. This young man had come from a lifestyle of drug and alcohol addiction that had landed him in jail. That night the Lord spoke to me and told me that there was going to be a baptism of the Holy Ghost and fire and that there would be some people in the meetings who were going to catch the anointing of the fire of God and be transformed.

That night, we were laying hands on people to receive the fire of God's Spirit. When I got to this young man and laid hands on him, the power of God hit him, and he began to violently speak in tongues and be touched by the power of God's Spirit. As he did, a transformation began to happen on the inside, and he caught the anointing of the fire of God. As he yielded to the fire of God, the Lord set him free from all sorts of bondages and things from his past like alcoholism, drugs, and a lifestyle of promiscuity and perversion. He was never the same. Within a few months, he sensed that God had spoken to him about moving to San Diego, where we are based, and to do an internship with us and serve the ministry.

Within a year and a half, this young man had already had many invitations to speak at youth groups and preach on mission trips. He is a prime example of what God can do in someone's life if he or she will yield to the fire of God's presence and obey His voice. This young man went from a lifestyle of bondage and defeat, always drinking, doing drugs, and being in trouble with the law, to a place of total freedom by God's Spirit. Now he is seeing God use him powerfully in signs, wonders, and miracles in the streets as well as in different nations and churches. Also, he has been a powerful example to the young people around him of walking out a lifestyle of purity, no compromise, and love. There have been many young people who have caught the fire that is on his life and now are becoming Burning Ones as well.

Another awesome thing is that not only does this young man thrive in ministry, but he is also now a manager of a very famous restaurant chain and is being used by God mightily in the marketplace as well. I believe that within a few years we will see this young man begin to step into a place of full-time ministry as a revivalist to the nations as he continues to grow and mature.

How Do We Practically Embrace the Fire of God?

The first thing to do is ask God for His fire. The Bible says, "We have not because we ask not" (See James 4:2). It's time to cry out to God for more of His holy fire so we can walk just like Jesus did when He was in the earth. Matthew 7:7-8 reads:

> *Ask, and it will be given to you; seek, and you will find; knock, and it will be opened to you. For everyone who asks receives, and he who seeks finds, and to him who knocks it will be opened.*

True faith has action behind it. We must cry out continually for more of God's presence. Being filled with the Spirit of God is not just a one-time thing. It's a lifestyle.

There are things in each of our lives that hinder us from going deeper with God. We must get free from the things of the flesh as well as the spirit of this age. Part of our journey to becoming champions for God is to allow Him to set us free from mindsets and attitudes that hinder us from coming into a greater degree of His glory.

> *...Let us lay aside every weight, and the sin which so easily ensnares us, and let us run with endurance the race that is set before us, looking unto Jesus, the author and finisher of our faith, who for the joy that was set before Him endured the cross, despising the shame, and has sat down at the right hand of the throne of God* (Hebrews 12:1-2).

True freedom comes when we look to Jesus, when we stare right into His face—no matter where we have been or what we have done—when we despise the shame and move on. He has defeated the enemy, as well as sin, once and for all at the cross. God wants us to begin to position ourselves to receive the fire of God and to allow that fire to purge or refine us so that we can be Burning Ones who will carry the flame of His love to others around us.

No Shortcuts

I believe that God wants us to pay the price to walk in the anointing of the Holy Spirit and fire, and there are no shortcuts. You can try to walk around the fire or jump over the fire, but ultimately, you will discover that you can run, but you cannot hide. The Father will seek you out.

About nine months prior to me working on this book, I had a visitation in which the Lord spoke to me about the cost of the anointing. I was in Grand Junction, Colorado, visiting my family who lives there. During a time of prayer, I got caught up in a vision with God. In this experience, an angel appeared to me and handed me a large pearl. As I looked at the pearl the angel handed me, I noticed it was not a normal pearl by any means. The pearl he handed me was huge. In fact, it was like the size of softball, if not bigger. As the angel handed me this pearl, I noticed something else very different about it. The pearl was encased or surrounded by a flame of fire, and as he put it in my hands, I could feel the warmth of God's great love radiating from the pearl into my heart.

After I spent a few moments looking at this beautiful pearl, the experience ended, and God immediately began to speak to me about the meaning of this vision. He said, "Son, now is the time that I am releasing the precious things of My Kingdom, the things that no eye has seen, no ear has heard, and no mind or heart has conceived. But I want you to tell My people this: There are no shortcuts in this next season. They must pay the price to walk in the precious things of My Kingdom. They must embrace the fire of My presence in order to access greater realms of authority and power in the Spirit. In fact, they must become like the merchant in the Bible who gave all to obtain the pearl of great price. I want My people to know that if My Son Jesus had to pay a price to walk in the precious things of God while He was on the earth, then how much more do the people of God need to pay that same price?"

After God spoke this to me, I was shocked. As I pondered all that He told me, I began to realize that what He said was true. Most of the Body of Christ has been crying out to God for more of His Kingdom, power, and glory, but most are not fully willing to pay the price necessary to walk in the precious things of the Kingdom. I began to think about the culture of our day and how a lot of people spend most of their time going from meeting to meeting trying to get the man or woman of God to lay hands on them for an impartation of God's Spirit. As I thought about this, I realized that this was the reason why most people don't walk in the supernatural power of God and have encounters with the Lord. They are running around trying to get impartation from others instead of just going to God themselves and paying the price of spending time with Him.

Then I began to think about the parable the Lord mentioned to me. He said that we must become like the merchant in the Bible who gave all to receive the pearl of great price. Let's look at this parable. Matthew 13:45-46 reads:

> *Again, the kingdom of Heaven is like a merchant seeking beautiful pearls, who, when he had found one pearl of great price, went and sold all that he had and bought it.*

As I read over this parable, I began to see what the Lord was talking about. It says that when the merchant found a pearl of great price, he gave *all to obtain* that pearl.

If we are to obtain the treasures or the precious things of God's anointing, there is a price to pay. God is looking for those who are willing to give all for the things of the Kingdom, those who will sell out and pay the price of intimacy with Him by spending time in His Word and presence, as well as allowing God to remove the things that hinder us from more of Him. God is looking for those who will value the precious things of His Kingdom above all else in this world and sell out in their relationship with Him to get them.

Part of walking with God and embracing His fire is commitment to intimacy with Him. If we will be faithful to make getting to know Him the first goal in our lives, He will bless us. Second Chronicles 16:9 tells us:

> *For the eyes of the LORD run to and fro throughout the whole earth, to show Himself strong on behalf of those whose heart is loyal to Him....*

To become mighty champions who are carriers of the flame of God's love, we must spend time with Him in His presence. It's in His presence that we are changed. When we spend time with the Lord in His presence, there is what I like to call a divine exchange. As we spend time with the Holy Spirit, He will set us on fire, because He is fire, and He will cause us to become pure because He is pure.

Have you have ever heard the phrase, "Who you hang around with is who you become"? There is truth in this statement. Who you hang out with you will become like. *"The LORD your God is a consuming fire, a jealous God"* (Deut. 4:24). If you will begin to spend time with God in His presence and ask Him for the fire of God, it will begin to rub off on you. It is impossible to spend time in the manifest presence of God and not be changed.

One of my favorite Kingdom quotes is by my friend and mentor, Bobby Conner. He says, "The anointing of God is more caught then taught." If you start to hang around with God and spend time in the fire of His presence, you will become like Him, and He will pass to you the torch of His presence. Then you will begin to walk with Him in resurrection life and power just as Jesus did as He walked the earth. The key to the power of God is found in intimacy with Him.

If Jesus had to separate Himself from the culture of His day and spend time with His Father listening to the voice of God in order to be effective in His mission on earth, then how much more do we need to do the same? And if Jesus had to spend time in the wilderness undergoing the fire of God and being tempted and tried by the enemy, then so do we.

There is a price to pay for the authority and power of God. Most churches like to talk about the baptism of the Holy Spirit, and they like to highlight the portion of Scripture found in Mark 1:9-11, when Jesus is baptized in the Jordan River by John and the Holy Spirit comes out of Heaven in the form of a dove and rests upon Him. But not many like to talk about what happened immediately after Jesus received this baptism.

As a Church, we like to focus on what is commutable regarding the Holy Spirit, but not the Holy Spirit and fire. The very next thing that happened to Jesus after He had the heavens open over His life and heard the voice of His Father say, *"This is My Son in whom I am well pleased,"* is that the Spirit of God drove Him into the wilderness to be tested in the fire. And He emerged as one who was on fire for God, a Burning One, catching the hearts of others on fire who said, *"Did not our heart burn within us while He talked with us on the road, and while He opened the Scriptures to us?"* (Luke 24:32).

What Happens After You Embrace the Fire

Once you have embraced the fire of God, you will have access to the glorious things of God. You become a Burning One carrying the torch of His love and releasing its flame everywhere you go—setting people free from the snares of the enemy by demonstrating God's great love through signs, wonders, and miracles.

I embraced the fire, and I still do. I have sought to walk as closely with the Lord as I humanly can. God makes up the rest. He doesn't call us to be perfect. He calls us to be with Him, and He invites us along to see what He is doing and to do what we see the Father doing.

One of the things the Lord spoke to me as a personal promise regarding the message of the torch of His love was that everywhere that I preached this message we would see notable, remarkable miracles that would confirm His word. He also told me that everywhere I would go I would see the real baptism of fire in our meetings because I had been faithful to spend time with God in His presence. The first place that I went to minister after I had this encounter was Auckland, New Zealand. We were there with our good friends Pastors Tim and Xenia Stevens for three nights of ministry as well as some daytime meetings at Horizon Church.

As we began the meetings on the first night, I preached the message on the torch, and God's fire fell. As I preached on the fire, the fire of God began to baptize people without anyone laying hands on anyone. Then the power of God started to move in the building. All of a sudden, people began to shake and cry out in tongues as the fire of God began to fall. As this was happening, one woman got touched by the fire of God and began to roll around on the ground. As she did, I had a word of knowledge from God that He wanted to heal someone who was totally deaf in one ear.

As I heard God speaking this word of knowledge to me, I spoke it out in the microphone and said, "God just spoke to me and told me that there is someone here tonight who is totally deaf in one ear, and He wants to heal them. Who is this person? If you have this condition, come up to the front so I can pray for you."

A man who was sitting on the first row yelled from the left side of the room. He began to yell and point at the woman who had been rolling around on the ground under the power of God who I had mentioned earlier, so I walked over to see what he was saying. As I got over to him, I put the microphone to his mouth so that the whole meeting could hear what he had to say. As I did, he told me that his wife was the one who was rolling around on the ground under the power of God and that she was born totally deaf in one ear. I went over to her with the microphone and stopped her from rolling around and asked her if God had healed her deaf ear.

She began to cry out, "I'm healed. I'm healed!" Everyone in the place went wild praising God. After everyone calmed down from praising God, I interviewed the woman and asked her why she was deaf. She told me that she was born with a deformed eardrum and that the doctors said it would be impossible for her to ever hear in her whole life. The result of her testimony was amazing. God's fire and love began to move throughout the room and heal people without anyone laying hands on them.

Then later that night, we prayed for a woman who had been in a car accident and had broken her ankle. As we prayed for her, God melted several metal pins the doctors used to fuse her ankle bones back together after the car accident. She could physically feel the metal pins protruding out of her ankle before we prayed, and after we prayed, she could not find the metal pins anymore, and all of the pain that was in her ankle was gone. Jesus did a creative miracle. He replaced the metal pins with brand new bones and ligaments.

All weekend long, the fire of God's love fell and people were being healed. One of the strangest miracles that happened that weekend was a miracle that God did for a 20-year-old woman. As we were praying for the sick, God gave me a word of knowledge and told me that He wanted to heal someone who had an issue with a hernia. As I gave this word of knowledge in the meeting and invited anyone who had the condition to come down for prayer, a young woman came down and said that she had just had surgery done a few weeks before our meetings on a severe hernia. She had been lifting something very heavy at her work when a part of her intestine popped out of her stomach lining and she had to undergo emergency surgery. As a result, the doctors had to cut her open in her lower stomach area to fix the problem.

As she came to the meeting, she was still hurting because of the surgery, and you could see that, even as she walked up to get prayer, she was in pain and walking slowly. As we prayed for her, the fire of God hit her and she was instantly healed. She testified in the meeting that all the pain had left her body. Later, the pastors told me that the woman said that not only did God heal her from the pain of the surgery regarding the hernia, but He also removed the scar. The scar from where the doctors cut her open from surgery was completely gone. She said that the area that had been cut open had no appearance of any kind of the surgery being done and that the skin was like brand new baby skin.

After this awesome weekend in God's fiery presence, I realized that I had definitely caught something of a new level of God's power and fire from the encounter that I had with the torch of His love. As I thought about this, I realized that when we encounter God's fire and presence, we are changed. We saw a greater level of glory that weekend in New Zealand than we had all year round.

One of the things that will happen when we become carriers of the torch of His love is that we will see the fires of revival move in people's lives to revive them and to set people free from sickness and disease.

So how do you become one who is on fire? It happens by embracing the fire of God personally. Let Him touch your mind, body, and spirit and transform you. God wants to release you from everything that has come against you—drugs, alcohol, pornography, promiscuity, the wounds from others who have shredded your heart and life, and the damage the enemy has done to your family. He wants to burn it out of you. And then you will be free to pass on the healing power and love of Jesus to all you meet.

BURNING QUESTIONS

Have you ever felt the outpouring of His love come upon you personally? Ask Him for an encounter with the Holy Spirit that will release a revelation of His love to you. What is it that stands in the way, that blocks you from receiving that encounter? Ask God to show you, and then let it go. And finally, ask the Holy Spirit to come and baptize you with fire and love.

Your Response

_____

_____

_____

_____

_____

_____

_____

_____

_____

_____

_____

_____

_____

_____

_____

_____

_____

_____

A Prayer to Get You There

You, oh Lord, are a good and loving God. You don't call us to give love away until we first know Your love, empowering us to become so filled with love that we cannot help but give it away to others. I ask You to baptize me in the fire of Your love. Set me up for a God encounter, and move me to the place where it can happen. Come here and reveal Yourself now or tell me where to go so I can experience You and Your presence more powerfully. I surrender all that stands between me and You. Let Your perfect love erase all my fears. I want You. I want to be transformed. I want to become one with You. Come, Holy Spirit!

CHAPTER 4

ROAR WITH AUTHORITY

S o the fire was hot. I warned you.

I'm sure the cave looks more appealing than moving forward into unknown territory. Once you have decided to leave your cave and embrace the fire, what's next? Get ready for a supernatural anointing to take you beyond your natural abilities. It's commissioning time! God commissions Burning Ones to become dread champions who roar with authority, run with supernatural ability, and defeat the enemy's plans.

You are no longer that person who was hidden away. There is no turning back. Dread champions don't retreat to their caves. They don't sink into despair over the piles of debt in their lives. They let go of their self-defeating thoughts and the negative words that others put upon them to weigh them down. They don't run away from the fire; they leap through the flames and emerge stronger than ever before. They roar with all that is within them, and their roar breaks off every hindrance and enables them to become more supernaturally empowered than they ever dreamed.

How do you shift from being someone who barely can stand to leave the cave and go to a church meeting (or hides away in the cave of church) to one who burns with God's love and power and moves out to the streets like a warrior on a mission, like a mighty man of David—a champion who is dreaded and feared by the enemy?

Let's look at the metaphorical language of the mighty men of David. At some point, they experienced an empowering that forever changed their perspective. The Bible moves from describing these guys as debt-ridden, discouraged nobodies into suddenly calling them mighty men of valor who had faces like lions and feet that were swift like gazelles and were experts with the shield, spear, and bow. The Word also tells us that the least of these men could slay hundreds of men at one time and the mightiest of these warriors could slay a thousand enemy soldiers with one sword and not be touched. These men also had a supernatural ability to scale or leap over a wall and run down their enemies by the power of God (see Ps. 18:29).

ANOINTED LIONS AND LIONESSES

I believe that the reason these men are described as fierce warriors who had faces that looked like lions is because they looked like their God. They had been so transformed into the likeness of their King that they reflected His nature and image.

They beheld Jesus as the Lion, and they started to look like Him. After all, He is called *"the Lion of the tribe of Judah"* (Rev. 5:5). Lions are known as a symbol of authority and kingship. They have been referred to as the kings of the jungle for good reason; when a lion roars, every creature in the jungle can hear the sound and stand alert. It is said that the roar of a lion can travel up to two to three miles in distance, and if you are close enough to a roaring lion, you can even feel the earth shake beneath you. The roar of the lion is known to bring the dread, or sudden terror, of the lion upon every creature in the jungle when they hear the sound of its roar. In some cases, it can even cause animals to panic and run. Just like in the natural animal kingdom, when the Lion of Judah (or His sons and daughters) roars, all who hear it recognize the Lion's superior power and authority.

The King of Glory, the Lion of Judah, is about to roar! When He does, all in this world will see and know His authority, and it will send a sudden fear or panic upon His enemies. God wants the nature of the Lion of the tribe of Judah to be seen upon His people. He wants to begin to display His authority and kingship through their lives just like the mighty men of David. I believe it is a picture of what God is about to do with His people in this day and hour. He is about to raise up a people of boldness and faith who won't run from the opposition of the enemy, but will face it with great faith and courage.

The Bible says that Jesus Christ, the hope of glory, is alive on the inside of us (see Col. 1:27). Jesus is the Lion of the tribe of Judah, so that means that the nature of the Lion is alive in us as well. The Lion of the tribe of Judah is alive inside of us, and He wants the same boldness that He has to be seen through us. *"The wicked flee when no one pursues; but the righteous are bold as a lion"* (Prov. 28:1). In fact, He wants to put an anointing of might upon our lives that we would destroy the works of darkness everywhere we go, just like David and his mighty men did in their day.

SWIFT LIKE GAZELLES

One of the other markers of dread champions is that they will have feet like gazelles—referring to their supernatural acceleration. God is going to cause those who are willing to pay the price of intimacy with Him to become champions who will step into an anointing of supernatural acceleration and power. They will have a supernatural ability to run hard and not faint. They will be able to leap over the highest walls of opposition just like a gazelle can leap a large fence with no problem in the natural. They will also walk in an anointing where they will always seem to be one step ahead of the enemy, ultimately gaining the victory.

The life of Elijah, one of God's dread champions, gives us a prime example of this acceleration. First Kings 18:20-45 tells the story of how Elijah called down fire from Heaven to confront the prophets of Baal, positioning God's power as superior over the enemies of God. He climbed to the top of Mount Carmel to cry out to God to send rain in the time of drought. King Ahab followed him up the mountain to see what would happen. He called on God six times to send rain. Each time, Elijah asked his servant to check to see if there were any clouds in the sky. There was not a cloud in sight after six times of prayer. The seventh prayer brought a report about a cloud the size of a man's fist appearing in the sky. That was enough for Elijah. A small beginning was about to become a downpour.

He knew to get off the mountain before the rain stopped him, and he started running. Ahab was wise enough to hitch up his chariot and begin his way down the mountain as well. Who can outrun a chariot? First Kings 18:46 tells us about a supernatural empowerment that came upon Elijah: *"Then the hand of the LORD was on Elijah, and he girded up his loins and outran Ahab to Jezreel"* (NASB).

Dread champions are positioned to be empowered beyond their natural abilities. Champions will have an ability to always be one step ahead of their enemies. God can accelerate us to run ahead of the religious spirit of our day. Ahab represented the religious spirit. He was not a godly man by any means. He was married and submitted to Jezebel—the evil queen of the land. This story is an example of how the champions that God is raising up today will have an ability to always outrun the religion of their day.

Dread champions will have feet like gazelles, and they will be able to leap over the walls of opposition and run faster than the enemy, and their supernatural abilities will cause people to take notice. However, the weapons that they carry will cause the enemy to tremble and the oppressed to rejoice.

Experts With Weapons

One of the things we must understand is that as Christians, the weapons of our warfare are not carnal, but are mighty in God to the pulling down of strongholds. I don't believe God is asking us to kill people with swords, shields, and bows in our time and day. I believe all of this talk about the way the mighty men of David looked, as well as the way they fought, is metaphorical for us to learn how to battle against the enemy in our time and day. It's a blueprint to walk in victory over the devil and all of his plans. Old Testament champions fought with natural weaponry that was supernaturally empowered. We fight with supernatural weapons that are God-inspired to us—weapons called "the Word" and the "Holy Spirit." They become our sword, bow, and shield.

When we have a value for the Word and the Spirit, acceleration of supernatural power happens. God is raising up people who are going to be experts with the shield, the sword, and the bow.

THE SHIELD OF FAITH AND
SWORD OF THE SPIRIT

One of the marks of the dread champions is that they will be experts with the shield and with the sword. These two weapons go hand in hand. If you carry one without the other, you will become vulnerable to the attacks of the enemy and could be easily defeated. God wants us to begin to understand how to be victorious over the enemy and his ways of warfare that come against our lives. Let's first look at the sword.

Hebrews 4:12 tells us that the sword is the Word of God:

> For the word of God is living and powerful and sharper than any two-edged sword, piercing even to the division of soul and spirit, and of joints and marrow, and is a discerner of the thoughts and intents of the heart.

If we are going to do mighty things for God, we must know His Word. The Word of God is like a sword in times of battle with the enemy, and it gives us the ability to discern what is of God and His Kingdom and what's not.

Now let's look at the shield, which is faith. In Ephesians 6:16, Paul mentions the *"shield of faith"* that will enable you to extinguish all the flaming arrows of the evil one. The purpose of this shield of faith is to stop the words and attacks of the enemy that come against you. When you combine the sword of God's Spirit and the shield of faith, you stop the words of the enemy from impacting your thoughts and replace them with the word of the Lord telling you who you are and how to proceed with the mission before you.

The way the devil attacks us is in our thought lives. What he tries to do is shoot arrows of fear, doubt, and deception at us. The devil is the author of deception, and what he tries to do is trick us into believing lies about ourselves, or even God, as well as God's Word, in order to gain ground on us in the spirit and rob us of our God-given authority, as well as our destiny.

We must use our weapons of warfare against the devil to overcome him and his attacks. We must use God's Word, which is the sword of the Spirit, to be able to discern what is of God and what is of the devil. We must also combine the sword with the shield of faith by truly believing that God's words and promises are real in and over our lives.

Paul the apostle taught on spiritual warfare and gave us keys to overcome the devil's attacks in the spirit.

> For though we walk in the flesh, we do not war accord-
> ing to the flesh. For the weapons of our warfare are
> not carnal but mighty in God for pulling down strong-
> holds, casting down arguments and every high thing
> that exalts itself against the knowledge of God, bringing
> every thought into captivity to the obedience of Christ,
> and being ready to punish all disobedience when your
> obedience is fulfilled (2 Corinthians 10:3-6).

When you combine God's Word with faith in what God's Word says, you will be able to overcome the works of the flesh as you take captive every thought and temptation of the devil and cause it to come under obedience to what the Word of God says. You can see this in the life of Jesus when He was tempted by satan in the wilderness. The enemy tried to attack Jesus by getting into His head and challenging His security as the Son of God, trying to reinterpret His knowledge of God's Word and sway His loyalty to God in worship.

How did Jesus fight? Jesus took the shield of faith and the sword of the Spirit to discern and overcome the devil's lies and deceptions. Matthew 4:3-4 gives us a clue as to how Jesus wielded the sword:

> *Now when the tempter came to Him, he said, "If you are the Son of God, command that these stones become bread."*
>
> *But He [Jesus] answered and said, "It is written, Man shall not live by bread alone, but by every word that proceeds from the mouth of God."*

In this scene, Jesus easily defeated the enemy by being secure in knowing who He is as the Son of God. Jesus fought with the sword of the Word and quoted the Scriptures, reminding satan who He is. When that didn't work, the devil went on to try to tempt Jesus again. Matthew 4:5-7 tells us that the devil took Jesus up to the holy city, set Him on the pinnacle of the temple, and said to Him:

..."If you are the Son of God, throw yourself down. For it is written: 'He shall give His angels charge over you,' and, 'In their hands they shall bear you up, lest you dash your foot against a stone.'"

Jesus said to him, "It is written again, you shall not tempt the LORD your God."

This time satan tried a different tactic. He tried to shoot an arrow of deception at Jesus regarding the Word of God, but Jesus raised the shield of faith and unleashed a blow back at the devil with the sword of the Spirit as He correctly discerned the deception of the enemy and quoted the truth of God's Word back at him. The devil will come with the appearance of being right, but it does not mean that he is right.

The devil is the author of deception, and one of the ways he tries to deceive and derail Christians is by perverting God's Word. He tries to twist God's Word and your mind into thinking satan's interpretation is correct. That's why it is so important to possess the sword of God's Spirit and build a strong foundation of the Word of God in your life.

The last area of attack the devil tried regarded worship. He took Jesus up on an exceedingly high mountain and showed Him all the kingdoms of the world and their glory and tempted Him by telling Him he would give Jesus all that He saw if He would just bow down and worship him. Jesus finished the devil off as he stated: *"Away with you, Satan! For it is written, 'You shall* *worship the L*ORD *your God, and Him only you shall serve'"* (Matt. 4:10).

Then the devil left Him—the temptation was over. He was defeated by the shield of faith—which is knowing who you are in Christ. He was overcome by the word of truth—which is knowing who He is to you.

The devil is after our intimacy and our sonship with God (which applies to both sons and daughters), as well as our knowledge of God's Word and our worship of Him. If we can overcome in these three areas of attack—with the sword of the Spirit and the shield of faith—we will become victorious over the devil and all of his power, and like Jesus, we will shut him down and he will flee from us.

THE BOW AND ARROW

Let's discuss the bow and arrow. Just like with the sword and the shield, the bow and arrow that we are talking about here are not natural weapons, but spiritual ones. It's not talking about something we pull back with our hands to launch arrows in the air with. It's talking about our decrees and prayers to God that we speak forth in faith—decrees that are like mighty arrows that strike God's enemies down as we declare His Word and promises over our lives in the spirit realm. Prayer is the bow of the Lord and positions us for launching arrows.

When we begin to pray in the Spirit, we begin to access this weapon of warfare. It is then combined with decrees—the arrows that are launched into the spirit realm during our times of prayer. As we pray and hear the voice of God, He speaks to us about the words/arrows to shoot. The arrows are the promises of God as well as His Word or voice, and when we position ourselves in prayer and hear and decree what God tells us, our warfare in the Spirit becomes effective. Game over. The arrows of God's Word cause strongholds to crumble.

Job 22:28 says, *"You will also decree a thing, and it will be established for you; so light will shine on your ways"* (NASB). As we decree things in the Spirit, we see the light of God's glory move and work on our behalf.

The Burning Ones whom God is equipping in this hour will become dread champions like David's warriors—those who are experts in hearing the voice of God and decreeing the victory into existence.

Commissioned for Breakthrough

I believe that we are in a season when God wants to commission us for breakthrough. The anointing of God on our lives is not so much about us; it's about them. The world has some giants coming against it. People are facing giants of sickness and disease, and the Scripture tells us that healing is the children's bread—our right, purchased at the cross by Jesus' blood (see

Isa. 53:4). Cities face giants of bankruptcy, and the Scripture says that wisdom and strategy of the Holy Spirit are yours for the asking (see James 1:5). Countries face poverty and war and giants who come to the door and decimate villages when the Scripture says that dread champion peacemakers will arise and miracles will be released that will break through the evils of suffering (see Acts 13:47).

God wants us to step up and be commissioned for breakthrough. He wants us to recognize that we have been born for *"such a time as this"* (Esther 4:14) The question is, what does the commissioning involve? Let's look further at the life of David.

David carried a powerful anointing of breakthrough. He once slew a lion and a bear as they attacked his sheep, and then he went on to take out the most-feared giant in the land, Goliath. While everyone was afraid to face this Philistine, David, a very young man at the time, got angry. He made a decree that he would kill the giant. He was confident in God. He knew that he had killed the wild beasts of nature before as the supernatural ability of the Holy Spirit came upon him. He knew that, when he felt that supernatural ability, that sense of God's strong presence upon him, God was with him and he would win. David, simply through long days spent in solitude with God, worshiping Him on the mountains, knew how to partner with God to accomplish His will. He was perfect in the timing of his actions, and God directed his aim.

David did not have a struggle in his fight against Goliath. David took him out with one smooth stone and one sling of his slingshot, and it was over. David had stepped into a "breaker anointing." A breaker anointing gets maximum results with very little effort. God wants to teach us to become dread champions who feel His presence and know His timing and are so close to Him that we release breakthrough to slay giants one at a time.

In Isaiah 10:27, we see that it is the anointing that breaks the yoke. God wants to anoint us with a breaker anointing so we won't have to work and toil by the sweat of our own brows to do things for Him, but that breakthrough would happen instantly.

Psalm 29:1-5 gives us many keys to walking in this breaker anointing as well as the Lion of Judah anointing of dominion that I have been talking about.

> Give unto the LORD, O you mighty ones, give unto the LORD glory and strength. Give unto the LORD the glory due to His name; worship the LORD in the beauty of holiness. The voice of the LORD is over the waters; the God of glory thunders; the LORD is over many waters. The voice of the LORD is powerful; the voice of the LORD is full of majesty. The voice of the LORD breaks the cedars, yes, the LORD splinters the cedars of Lebanon.

In this Scripture, you can see that David is talking to his mighty ones. I believe that he is teaching them how to walk in a breaker anointing as well as giving them keys to stay humble and see the mighty hand of God move on their behalf. You can see this breaker anointing unfold. In this verse, you see the power of God's voice. David describes God's voice as majestic and powerful and says the God of glory thunders over the earth with His voice. Then he shows us in this psalm the power of God's voice to shatter strongholds; the voice of the Lord breaks the cedars and splinters the cedars of Lebanon. Lebanon represents the works of the flesh. So another way of saying what David is talking about is that the voice of the Lord breaks or splinters the works of the flesh. What are the works of the flesh? The works of the flesh are sin, sickness, disease, poverty, and anything else that opposes the blessings of God.

Remember in the New Testament when Jesus laid hands on the 70 disciples and sent them out, and they came back to Him rejoicing in the awesome miracles they had seen? As they did, Jesus said to them, *"I saw Satan fall like lightning..."* (Luke 10:18). When the God of glory began to thunder from Heaven, the enemies of God and their strongholds began to fall down to the ground. God is raising up a company of dread champions who will destroy and displace the works of the flesh and darkness everywhere they go. We have seen many times when God begins to thunder on behalf of His Word from Heaven, and at times we have even seen the mighty hand of God release tangible evidence and even signs in the natural that He has dealt with enemy strongholds. It is the manifold wisdom of God that deals with the principalities and spiritual strongholds of the enemy in the land (see Eph. 3:10).

As we speak God's Word or release the prophetic voice of God through prayers, decrees, and prophecy, the strongholds of the enemy begin to break.

DREAD CHAMPIONS ROAR
AND THE EARTH RESPONDS

In January of 2010, my wife and I were hosting a conference in San Diego, California, called DECREE. On the last night of the event, the Lord instructed us to go into a time of high praise and prophecy. So corporately, we began to go into an intense time of praise and worship unto God. God's glory presence began to get heavy and weighty, to the point that some could not stand in the room. We began to make decrees in this spirit over southern California. Several of our guest speakers and I began to prophesy as the Lord led. We also gave various words over the people attending the meetings as well as over the region of San Diego and even the state of California. As we did this, the voice of the Lord began to come very clear to us.

One of the things I began to declare under the spirit of prophecy was that God was going to open up the floodgates of Heaven and cause the rain of revival to fall across southern California again. As I spoke this, I went into a vision, and I began to see spinning winds or whirlwinds in the spirit that looked like tornados of God's glory. The Holy Spirit spoke to me and said, "Ecclesiastes 1:6." Quickly, I turned to the passage to see what it said. It lined up with what God was showing me in the spirit. It read: *"The wind goes toward the south, and turns around to the north; the wind whirls about continually, and comes again on its circuit."* As God began to show this to me, out of my belly came a continuation of the prophecy.

I began to prophesy that God was going to soon birth another Jesus movement in southern California and cause a second wave of counterculture revival to be seen all across California. This wave would then spread throughout the United States of America. As I was speaking this out, I found myself saying that God was going to send the whirlwinds of His Spirit and the rains of Heaven to deal with the strongholds of the enemy in the land. In addition, God was going to release a natural sign that He was dealing with the strongholds in the spirit realm that had prevented this second Jesus movement from coming into the land. God would prepare the spiritual atmosphere of southern California for revival again. Then I read Ecclesiastes 1:6 and declared that God would release it.

This all took place on a Saturday night, the last night of our event.

Within two days, God begin to confirm the word in the natural. On Monday, the winds in the natural began to pick up and blow in a very unusual manner in San Diego, as well as the whole southern California region. Just like the Scripture in Ecclesiastes 1:6 said, the winds began to blow toward the south and ended up reaching up to 90 miles an hour. During the next few days, it began to violently rain in southern California, and three tornados ended up touching down in the southern California region. The winds even shifted after a few days, and the storm blew up toward northern California and the rains and tornados were seen up there as well.

Everything happened just as the Scripture I had quoted when I prophesied said. The winds blew to the south, which in San Diego as well as most parts of southern California is not normal, as the winds tend to come up from the south and blow to the north. That week the state of California had over five tornados (when it is a rare event to even have one tornado) and more rain in a single week than it had received in the previous year.

The God of glory thundered over us that week, and I believe it cleared a way for revival to happen in southern California again. The key to this move of God happening was two things; both of them are found in Psalm 29. The first was that we all went into a time of intense worship and praise, and then we began to release God's voice through prophecy. If we learn to worship the Lord in the beauty of holiness and declare what He is saying, He will thunder on our behalf and splinter the strongholds of the enemy. The key is worship and hearing God's voice.

DEVELOPING THE ROAR OF LOVE

Now let's look more at Psalm 29 and grab a hold of the keys in this Scripture to enter into a breaker anointing. There are several things in this portion of Scripture that I want to highlight. The first is that intimacy with God and obedience to His Word will manifest the authority and power of God. It was as we were obedient to declare the Word of God that the strongholds shook in southern California. Before we see any mention of the manifestation of God's power in this Psalm, we see several things mentioned that will lead up to this breaker anointing being manifested.

The first key to developing the roar of love that releases a breaker anointing is worship and praise—the sounds of the roar of love.

Like I said earlier, if we are going to carry the nature of the Lion of the tribe of Judah, we will have to know how to have true intimacy with God. I believe the mighty men of David had faces like lions because it was symbolic for what the dread champions whom God is raising up would look like. It is also something of a metaphorical language meant to teach us more about these mighty champions. I believe that God is about to raise up a generation of lovesick worshipers of the King. They will release violent praise and love for God that causes them to walk in the nature of the Lion of the tribe of Judah. Judah means praise. I believe that as we give God glory, honor, and true praise, we will begin to tap into this anointing of the breaker.

The first key to tapping into the breaker anointing is found in Psalm 29:1-2. In these verses, we really see the heart of who David was and the intimacy that he carried with God that enabled him to walk in a breaker anointing that ripped down the strongholds of the enemy.

> Give unto the LORD, O you mighty ones, give unto
> the LORD glory and strength. Give unto the LORD

the glory due to His name; worship the LORD *in the beauty of holiness.*

The first key we must recognize is that if we are going to walk as dread champions in the earth with a breaker anointing upon our lives, we must live in a place of true intimacy, worship, and humility before God. The first thing David says to his mighty ones is that they need to learn to give to the Lord the glory and strength that's due to His name. The second is to worship the Lord in the beauty of holiness. If we are to access this realm of the breaker that was upon David's life, as well as the nature of the Lion that we see in the lives of his mighty men, we must learn to give God the glory, strength, and worship that's due His name.

God will not share His glory with another. We must learn to give thanks to God for the mighty breakthroughs that God brings in our lives as well as thanksgiving and praise for allowing us to partner with Him in releasing the anointing of God. The requirement of walking in an anointing of breakthrough is knowing how to give God the glory and praise due His name while seeing His hand move through our lives to do mighty things for His name's sake.

THE ROAR OF AUTHORITY

The key to releasing a breaker anointing is found in hearing and releasing the voice of the Lord. In Psalm 29:3-5 we see this principle. Before there is any release of power, there is the voice of God.

> *The voice of the* LORD *is over the waters; the God of glory thunders; the* LORD *is over many waters. The voice of the* LORD *is powerful; the voice of the* LORD *is full of majesty. The voice of the* LORD *breaks the cedars, yes, the* LORD *splinters the cedars of Lebanon.*

The God of glory wants to thunder on our behalf. And He wants us to be those who release Heaven on earth—that when we pray, when we begin to release the decree of God, and when we begin to pray for the sick and do the things that Jesus did, the cedars of Lebanon are splintered and shattered.

The cedars of Lebanon represent the works of the flesh. God wants us to splinter sin, sickness, disease, poverty, shame, anger, fear, and all these different things that oppose the will of God. God wants to give us the keys to know how to walk in this anointing of David. The key, however, is to learn to tap into the voice of God. When we do what God says, breakthrough happens. So the question is, how do we tap into His voice? We draw closer to Him. We get to know Him and become so full of His presence that our voices and His voice become one, and we speak out what we hear Him saying. And as we speak and decree what we hear, prophecies come to pass.

Another key to the breaker anointing is worship and hearing God's voice. David said:

Give unto the LORD, oh you mighty ones, give unto the LORD glory and strength. Give unto the LORD the glory due His name; worship the LORD in the beauty of holiness (Psalm 29:1-2).

When you worship God in spirit and truth, when you worship Him in the beauty of holiness, you will start to hear the voice of God because it says the voice is over the waters.

Worship releases the waters, the rains, and the Holy Spirit because when we worship God, His cloud comes. And when the cloud comes, there is precipitation in the cloud, and it begins to rain down. It's the anointing of the waters of Heaven, and it's the Holy Spirit. And when we begin to receive the waters, when we begin to receive the rain, when we begin to encounter Holy Spirit, what does He do? He comes to teach us, He comes to show us, and He comes to speak to us of the things that the Father Himself is saying. And when we begin, in the atmosphere of worship, to make decrees of what God said, it will splinter and shatter the enemy's kingdom.

But what is it to worship the Lord in the beauty of holiness? If we want to walk in strength, glory, and power, we must learn to first worship Him. God wants to release more revelation to us on this because I don't think we understand what it truly is to worship the Lord in the beauty of holiness. So many people think that in church, we're worshiping God, but really we're just praising.

There is more to worship. In fact, I see three aspects to worshiping the Lord in the beauty of holiness—worship, praise, and thanksgiving. Those three aspects, I believe, combined together, are an expression of worshiping the Lord in the beauty of holiness. So many of us think we're worshiping God, and the reality is we're just praising Him. But praise is different than worship. Praise is singing songs to God, and worship is an attitude in our hearts toward God.

If we're going to understand what worship looks like, we have to look at the worship going on in Heaven. What does it look like? It's elders on their faces before the King, casting their crowns at His feet, saying, *"You are worthy, O Lord, to receive glory and honor and power; for You created all things, and by Your will they exist and were created"* (Rev. 4:11). A similar worship comes from the four living creatures, who also bow down and say, *"Holy, holy, holy, Lord God Almighty, who was and is and is to come"* (Rev. 4:8). Worship is more than just singing words to God; it's an attitude and posture of our hearts toward Him. It's truly recognizing that He is the King.

When was the last time you bowed down before the King, you—alone in your bedroom—when nobody's around? When was the last time you laid on your face before God just because He's worthy of praise? When you truly worship Him and recognize who He is, the holiness of God will be imparted to you. Why do you think the living creatures and elders are crying, "Holy, holy, holy"? It's because when you see God for who He really is, that's the natural response!

When we begin to worship the Lord in the beauty of holiness, the devil won't even want be near us, because we will carry that holiness with us from the throne.

Now let's talk about thanksgiving and praise. Thanksgiving and praise are powerful. Psalm 48:1 reads, *"Great is the LORD and greatly to be praised...."* When we praise God, we release the greatness of who He is, and it impacts the atmosphere everywhere we go. Praise will cause us to walk in triumph over the enemy, and it will cause us to walk victoriously in the unseen realms as well.

The champions God is raising up in this hour won't just be victorious over the devil, but they will triumph over him. There is a big difference between a triumph and a victory. A victory is the celebration of a battle that you just won, but a triumph is a celebration of a battle that has already been won. In other words, we are not just winning the battle against satan and his kingdom. We have already won the battle because of the blood of the lamb and His sacrifice.

God wants us to become victorious in all circumstances and trials. He wants us to scale the walls of opposition and slay our enemies with weapons of warfare that are not carnal, but are mighty in God to the ripping down of strongholds (see 2 Cor. 10:4). Psalm 106:47 tells us that the triumph of God is released as His people give Him thanks and praise. God is about to give to His people the keys to overcoming the enemy and all of his attacks. When we give thanks to God and praise Him for that which is to come, according to His promises, it releases breakthrough in every situation.

The Bible is full of stories where God thunders on behalf of His people with supernatural victories that were released through the high praises of God and giving thanks. The Lord wants to give us keys to scale or leap over the walls of opposition that we face in the day of battle with the enemy.

One of my fathers in the spirit, Bob Jones, says that the Body of Christ has to get over this syndrome of having an "itty-bitty God and a great big devil." There are too many people who live in a place of fear and defeat. It's as we praise and worship God that things come into right alignment. It's when we truly praise God that the enemy is put in his place, and we begin to walk in triumph over him. Praise will cause us to triumph over the devil.

Some might be asking, "What does it mean to triumph?" Paul the apostle talked about triumphing in the Lord in Second Corinthians 2:14 when he said, "*Now thanks be to God who always leads us to triumph in Christ....*" To fully understand what Paul is talking about here, we must look at what it was to triumph in the times of the Romans of his day.

To triumph in the time of the Romans meant that one king or ruler would overtake another king in battle. After the winning king captured the losing king, he beat him, stripped him naked, and put him in a cage for all to see. Then he took some of the losing king's most important men of war and government and chained them to the back of this cage. After this was done, the winning king attached the whole shackled crew to the back of a white chariot that was led by several white horses, jumped into the chariot, and dragged the cage throughout his city—a display that shouted triumph over the victory he won as people saw the enemies, humiliated and overcome, being dragged through the streets.

This is also a picture of what Jesus did to the devil at the cross, as well as a picture of what happens when we begin to praise God. Colossians 2:15 says that Jesus made a public spectacle of the devil, triumphing over him. When Jesus died and rose again, He stripped and defeated the devil, along with all of his principalities and powers, once and for all and disarmed them of their power and authority. That day, Jesus bound the devil and all of his evil forces, and now we get to triumph with Christ in this victory. God is inviting us to sit together with Him in His chariot of victory.

So now that you know what it is to triumph, you can see that whenever the devil raises his anger up against your life, you can just start praising God for the victory you have already received because of Jesus and watch as the devil retreats to the place where he belongs—bound in the cage that Jesus put him in, along with all his demons, principalities, and generals of war as they are shackled up in chains.

Psalm 149:5-9 is an example of how we triumph over the enemy through the high praises of God:

> *Let the saints be joyful in glory; let them sing aloud on their beds. Let the high praises of God be in their*

mouth, and a two-edged sword in their hand, to exe-cute vengeance on the nations and punishments on the peoples; to bind their kings with chains, and their nobles with fetters of iron; to execute on them the writ-ten judgment—This honor have all His saints....

This Scripture tells us that when the saints lift up the high praises of God in their mouths, it is like a two-edged sword that they fight with in the Spirit, and the kings of the earth are bound with fetters of iron, and we have access to release the written judgments of God upon the enemies of God.

The Roar That
Transforms Cities and Nations

One time when we were in Alberta, Canada, the Lord spoke to me in a dream through a song. In this dream, I heard the Spirit of the Lord say that He was releasing the double portion of Elijah and purity and intimacy across this land. As I went to this meeting, I knew exactly what I was supposed to preach because of my dream, so I preached on the spirit of Elijah.

Oddly, the Lord told me that He did not want me to move in miracles, but that He just wanted me to sing the song I had heard over the people that day. So I preached and released a word about the double portion of Elijah, and when it came time to close the meeting up, I asked everyone to stand and to praise God.

I stood up and sang that God was releasing the spirit of Elijah and purity and intimacy across the land. Then, after I proclaimed the song that God gave me in my dream, God spoke to me and told me to get the people to call down the fire of God upon the prophets of Baal. So we asked God for His fire to be released upon the prophets of Baal, and then we closed out the meeting.

Who are the prophets of Baal? They are not humans. It's not talking about people; it's talking about powers, principalities, and spiritual hosts of wickedness in heavenly places. And God has given us the keys today to bind those things, but we must be careful. We never want to just bind the devil or principalities over a region without hearing the voice of God. When we praise God, He will begin to speak to us, and when we decree what He says to do, breakthrough will happen.

So, what happened that morning in Alberta? After we closed out the meetings, we went out to lunch and found out that God had confirmed His Word with a sign in the natural. Within 30 minutes of singing the song and speaking the decree into the atmosphere, a hotel in that city that was overtaken by drug dealers, prostitutes, and pimps, and was a stronghold of lust and perversion in the city somehow caught on fire and burned to the ground. Nobody got hurt, but the stronghold in that city, a container of lust and perversion, a place where the work of the Baals had free reign, burned to the ground. It was a sign in the natural that God had done something in the heavenly realm because we were obedient to do what He said when He said to do it.

What you say and what you focus on are powerful. God is a big God who is able to do way more than you think. But He wants His sons and daughters to partner with Him in the task of transforming the world. He is calling you. He is holding out the sword of His Spirit and the shield of faith. Will you receive them? He is inviting you to take hold of His presence and learn how to move in Him, feeling the direction He is moving and inviting you to come along. He wants you to be so close to Him that wherever you go, you have a sense that He is with you, guiding you and directing you. His invitation is that His words would become your words.

BURNING QUESTIONS

What area in your life, work, or ministry do you need to see a breakthrough in? The Kingdom of God is something that needs to be taken like a dread champion—forcefully. Wimpish prayers don't cut it. Decrees based on His Word and prompted by His Spirit will shatter and scatter the enemy's opposition. Do you know how powerful you are when you move in intimate union with Jesus? What do you need breakthrough for in your life? Find the Scripture that promises victory and declare its fulfillment out loud.

Your Response

_____

_____

_____

_____

_____

_____

_____

_____

_____

_____

_____

_____

_____

_____

_____

_____

_____

_____

A Prayer to Get You There

Father, in the name of the Lord Jesus Christ,
I decree breakthrough in the area of

_____.

I declare Your word, the scriptural promise that says

_____.

And I thank You and praise You that You will
bring it to pass because I am Yours and You are
mine. I thank You for Your love, presence,
and power. Bring Your Kingdom!

CHAPTER 5

BURN ON

I have a friend named Annie who has been tapping into a creative anointing that seems to be changing others' lives. For the past few years, she often spends time in prayer asking God to show her things that He wants her to paint. Visions of people, places, or things come to mind, and she either draws or paints what she sees in prayer. One day, God gave her several visions of different people, so she simply drew and painted portraits of each one of them. By the time she was through, she had several paintings of people she had never seen or met stacked in her garage. Several weeks after finishing the paintings, she felt like the Lord told her to enter them into the art show of one of the biggest new age festivals in the country. So, off she went with a few fellow artists to set up a booth at the gathering.

The very presence of God burning in these Christian artists created a zone where God's presence was immediately felt by all who entered. A woman who was very famous in the new age world walked by Annie's booth and was surprised to find her face on one of the paintings that Annie had done weeks before.

As this woman studied the picture, she felt the presence of God come upon her, and she started crying. Knowing they had never met before, she asked Annie how Annie had known who she was. As a result, Annie now had an open door to share God's love with the woman, who was so touched by God that she gave her life to Jesus.

That week, several people entered the atmosphere of the booth and tent that my friend had set up. One woman came into the tent and told my friend that she could not connect to her spirit guides at all when she came into their tent. She went on to say that she felt an overwhelming sense of peace resting in the tent and wanted to know why—what kind of power did these artists possess? They explained that the power she felt was the presence of God. The woman immediately gained the revelation that God was real. They told her that it was a sign to her that God loved her.

Annie and her friends released the light of God in that place. They were Burning Ones. They were dread champions who were filled with boldness and moved into enemy territory, knowing they already had the victory. Annie and her friends were letting their lights shine in one of the darkest cultures in America. And when lights shine, darkness flees. Many people got physically healed and delivered that week in the tent as well.

Is Annie "just an artist"? Or is she one who is called to use her artistic abilities to seek and save the lost, to witness to the glory of God? God wants us to be set on fire so we can begin to let our lights shine so others in the world will take notice. He wants us to shine for His glory. In Matthew 5:16, Jesus said to let our lights shine so that the world would see and believe in God. No matter what field of work or art you are in or what you do to make a living, you have one distinct call—to let your light shine, not hide it. Burn on!

THE CREATIVE ANOINTING

The anointing of creativity has been released to many individuals throughout history and even more so in our day. God is using the arts—like painting, drama, dance, and music—to bring glory to His name. And people respond because they have a genuine hunger for anointed creativity in the world today. You can drive down most of the major streets of most major cities in America and find creative art centers or theaters. People seek out places to watch plays or art shows to unwind from the stress of the day. They are looking for something to inspire them and lift them higher.

If we recognize the significance of this anointing of creativity in our time and day to capture the heart of a generation that is lost and has no knowledge of who God is, we will bless creative expressions. We are living in a day when people are hungry for creativity. There is a huge rise in the number of people turning away from church, but following the New Age movements that focus on the arts and entertainment arena. God wants to anoint us as Christians to go into these movements of creativity as modern-day missionaries and show them the true creativity of the God who invented creativity.

People will stop before an anointed painting and suddenly weep as the presence of God washes them in His love. Viewers suddenly seeing a portrait of them that was painted by someone who has never met them take notice that God knows who they are and they are significant to Him. Street crowds will move toward musicians and dancers and watch the Burning Ones in action, lingering to hear about the Light of the world and watch a demonstration of His power. The arts are powerful.

God is going to invade today's society with the arts and invade the world of music. One of the strongest gifts that can be seen upon both the younger and older generation today is creativity that makes people stop and watch or listen. The Church must go after this anointing and make it theirs before the world does. In the days of Elvis Presley, the Church rejected the sound of rock n' roll, so the devil stole it, morphed it into new sounds that the world celebrated at Woodstock years later, and eventually drew the heart of a generation away from God. The Church has rejected great artists and dancers, turning their backs on the anointing of creativity, forcing those who would burn for God to flame out in the world. What if we welcomed the anointing for creativity?

Street performance seems to be one of the most anointed ways to captivate people's attention. When we are ministering in Africa, Indonesia, and other nations, we often rent flatbed trucks and a sound system, drive into towns or village squares, and blast some hip-hop music. Once, a whole team of 20 people performed a choreographed dance to the music in order to draw a crowd. Then after the performance, we called out words of knowledge for healing, demonstrated the power of God, and gave those watching a quick Gospel message—and then bam! Hundreds of people get saved, who would never stop to listen to our spoken message, simply because they are entertained for 10 minutes. God wants us to begin to be creative and use the gifts He has given the Church to glorify His name.

A few years ago, five of the top ten heavy metal bands in the secular arena were all led by born-again believers in Jesus Christ. Using their gifting and talents for the world to see, appearing on MTV music videos, and attending music award shows, they ended up using their fame to give honor and glory to God and giving voice to their generation. They are Burning Ones releasing light into the darkness. The Church may not appreciate their music, but the world takes notice of the gift and eventually realizes where that gift came from—Jesus.

While flying on a plane from Los Angeles to Seattle not too long ago, I had the blessing and privilege of sitting next to a rapper who was making it big in the secular music world. I could hear him talking on his cell phone before we took off. He was telling his friend that he was on his way to go to Seattle to sign a contract with a new record label. I couldn't help but listen since he sat so close, and I heard him say that some guy had just given him $150,000 for one of his CD projects. I was intrigued, so I started a conversation with him and asked him what he did for a living. He began to tell me that he was a rap/rock star who was using his career to give a positive message to this generation. Then he asked me what I did for a living, so I told him that I was a healing revivalist. He was fascinated and began to open up to me and ask all kinds of questions.

He ended up telling me that he was a Christian, too. Then he went on to tell me that he had just started to begin to make it big, and that one of his songs had just begun to get really good airtime on the radio and had hit number 1 for a bit. God had spoken to him to go into the secular arena and befriend rock stars and celebrities and give them Jesus, as well as bring a message of hope and love to the world in a nonreligious way. So for the past few years, that's what he has done.

He then went on to tell me about how some of the concerts and tours he was a part of were very dark, but how he and his wife would just go into the scene and love on people as they performed. Apparently, they were getting lots of opportunities to reach the unsaved and had gotten to share the love of God with a lot of the members of the secular bands they were touring with. God released a sign of His favor to the bands he was playing with, as well as to his record label managers, when they realized he was selling more albums as the opening band than the main bands who were better known. He said that the favor of God was being seen upon him and that people in the world were impressed. That favor was opening up bigger doors for him.

I was blown away and asked him if he had the support of a church or people praying for him. He told me that he was fully connected to a church and that the people in his church were blown away because of what God was doing with him. The coolest thing was that his pastor was fully backing him and telling him to go after secular music and be a light for Jesus for all to see. This guy's story is an example of what God is about to do with an entire generation. This guy is a true dread champion, boldly burning for all to see.

God wants to place Burning Ones in every part of society today with a supernatural anointing of the glory and favor of God upon their lives so that all who come into contact with them will see the fire of God's glory upon their lives.

Get ready to see Burning Ones releasing the Kingdom of God outside the Church in the areas of business, sports, arts, entertainment, government, religion, and education. God wants out of the box and is looking for Burning Ones who will show the world His glory by demonstrating the good works of the Kingdom of God in all areas of life.

We need to learn to recognize the gifts and callings that God has put in this generation. The reality is that there is a new generation of Burning Ones rising who will become dread champions for God in the earth. Some of these champions that God is going to raise up today are going to be movie stars and actors, artists, and performers. Others may be politicians, sports stars, businessmen and women, or even educators. God wants His people to let Him out of the box of only allowing God to rule and reign in the church building and allow Him to be seen through His people in everyday life.

PROPHETS TO GOVERNMENTS

I have a friend in Jakarta, Indonesia, named Constant (Nino) Ponggawa who is the owner of one of the most successful law firms in Indonesia. Some years ago, while spending time with God, he heard the Lord tell him that he was to run for a position in the Indonesian government in order to be a voice for God in his country. So in obedience to God, he ran for a position in parliament, God gave him favor, and he became one of 550 members of the Indonesian parliament.

Over the last five years, God has used him mightily to bring significant changes in political laws as well as to change the way the Indonesian government viewed Israel. A few years ago, when the Hamas Palestinians began to launch bombs at Israel, Nino realized that he was called to take a stand. Israel warned Hamas not to continue their attack, but they didn't listen. So Israel sent a powerful response aimed back at the Palestinians that caused much harm to the Palestinians and raised an international outcry against Israel.

God had previously spoken to Nino that there was coming a time when He wanted him to stand up for Israel in front of all of the members of the Indonesian government. When God said this, Nino became a little nervous. The majority of the members of the Indonesian government were Muslims who hated Israel and cursed them openly in parliament meetings.

In fact, at the time, Indonesia was so against Israel that on their national passports they printed, "No entry to Israel." Most of the members of the Indonesian parliament wanted Palestine to gain their freedom and independence from Israel. Nino watched the report about the bombings regarding Israel and Palestine, and he knew that when he went in the next day there was going to be a lot of harsh talk against Israel. Nino walked into the parliament meeting and people all over the room were yelling and cursing Israel. As Nino stood watching, the Lord spoke to him and said, "Remember I told you that I wanted you to speak up and defend Israel one day for Me? Today is the day that you are going to stand up for Israel to all of these men."

Nino's heart began to beat like crazy, and he thought, *Not now, Lord.* However, he felt the Lord tell him to push his buzzer to turn his microphone on to speak. So he went for it, and when he pushed the button and everyone saw that it was him who had pushed it, they all became quiet because they knew he was a Christian, and they wanted to hear what he had to say. As he began to speak, the Spirit of God took over. He found himself saying, "Palestinians need to have their independence and freedom, and we need to help them. Just like Indonesia was in captivity to the Dutch for over 300 years and wanted independence and got it, so should the Palestinians have freedom, and we are called to help them."

As he said this, the Muslims and the whole house of parliament were shocked that he, being a Christian, would espouse such a thing. He went on to say that Indonesia was called to be a peacemaker and that if they were going to maintain relationship with Palestinians and help them gain independence, then they would also have to maintain relations in a peaceful manner with Israel in order to help bridge the gap between the two for peace.[1]

The place went wild, and they all started arguing and yelling, "How can we make peace with Israel? We don't like Israel!" This was a bold and controversial thing for Nino to say at that time. It would have been like a member of the U.S. Senate standing up and taking a stand to make peace with Iraq or Afghanistan right after the terrorist attacks of 9/11.

Eventually, they all stopped fighting and went home. Afterward, the head of the parliament came up to my friend and told him he was crazy to stand up for Israel like that. Even though a lot of the members of parliament didn't agree with Nino about having relations with Israel at the time, they loved the idea that he wanted the Palestinians to gain independence and ended up respecting him for being bold and voicing his opinion.

Since the day that Nino took a stand for peace with Israel, things have improved regarding the government in Indonesia, and they are moving toward developing relations with Israel. Far less cursing toward Israel is going on in the parliament meetings, according to Nino. Another awesome thing that ended up happening shortly after that day that Nino spoke up for Israel was that Indonesia sent two members of parliament to represent Indonesia as a nation to a special meeting in the Middle East to discuss peace. One of the two members that ended up being selected by the entire Indonesian parliament to represent Indonesia on this matter was Nino. God used him to speak the wisdom of God into a seemingly impossible situation and then honored him by giving him a place to represent the nation of Indonesia on the very subject that he spoke up about. Also, since that day, Indonesia as a nation has taken several major steps toward positive relations with Israel, and they have now removed the quote that forbade entry to Israel from the passports.

Listen and Burn On

One of the things I want you to notice about these stories I am sharing with you is this: God spoke to the individuals to do something, and as they listened, they saw the supernatural hand of God moving in their midst. Intimacy with God and obedience to His voice manifest His Kingdom. You listen and you burn. You never know what might lie ahead of you as you step out in obedience to God's Word. When you are in the right place at the right time, anything can happen.

I have one friend whom God spoke to about going to Louisiana to help with disaster relief after Hurricane Katrina hit. He bought his ticket and went to help. Before he got on his plane, someone gave him a prophetic word about how he would not be able to go straight to the stadium in New Orleans, but God would open up a side door for him to get in. So he flew down and got to the Superdome in New Orleans—a chaotic scene full of shocked, sick, and traumatized people who had nothing. He tried to walk right into the front entrance of the building, but was stopped by some security guards who told him that he could not go in.

At first he was bummed about it, but then remembered the prophetic word he had received and realized that God had promised that he would open up a side door for him. So he went around the building and found another entrance on the side of the stadium, and those guards let him right in. It pays to be obedient to God. Once inside the stadium, he and another guy who was with him began to pray with people to be healed, and many miracles happened. They were able to share the love of God with many.

They kept walking further into the Superdome; all of a sudden they were stopped and told that they could not walk past a certain point because one of the most famous talk show hosts in America was doing a special report on the victims of Hurricane Katrina. As the security guards told them this, they saw the talk show host walking toward them. My friend heard the Lord say that he should tell the talk show host that God was going to give her back the red bike that was stolen from her when she was 5 years old. For a moment he thought, *I sure hope I am hearing right*, but even that bit of doubt didn't stop him. He boldly screamed out the talk show host's name and yelled, "God says that He is going to give you back the red bike that was stolen from you when you were 5 years old."

The security guards grabbed him to throw him out, but the startled talk show host yelled back, "Stop, let him go. What he is saying is true."

For about an hour, my friend got to speak into this woman's life. He told her that God loved her and that her show wasn't even the main calling on her life, but that God was going to use it as a platform to feed the hungry and house orphans. Tears streamed down her face as he talked with her. Wow, what an encounter that was. He thought that God was sending him to New Orleans just to pray for the Hurricane Katrina victims, and God opened a door for him to prophesy over the biggest talk show host in America. You never know what one act of obedience will open up. The Burning Ones God is raising up in this hour will be radically obedient to their Father's voice, and it will open up doors that no person could open and no person dare shut.

Burning Ones Light up the Night

God wants us to get out of the four walls of the church and begin to partner with Him to pour out His Spirit on all flesh. God wants us to begin to invade the enemy's strongholds and release the fire of His love in the darkest of places. He loves it when we light up the night with the light of God's glory.

Are you ready to carry revival outside of the church? Are you ready to burn on and light up the night with God's glory and invade the streets, bars, clubs, and college campuses?

Jesus was always hanging out with the tax collectors and the sinners of His day. He was known as a friend of sinners, and when He hung out with them, revival would break out. One time, when Jesus was hanging out at a tax collector's house, an entire city came to the door of the house to receive a touch from God, and He healed them all. Most of the environments Jesus brought revival to were not in the church; they were in people's homes, the streets, and among the so-called sinners of that day.

In Jakarta, Indonesia, one of the pastors who invited me to come rented out the most famous night club in Jakarta called The Equinox. He and his team felt that they needed to go into the darkness and bring the light, so they planned an evangelistic event in the darkest place they could think of and brought me in to be the main speaker. The Equinox has a huge reputation as a place where the partiers do drugs and even hook up to have sex. It is open six nights a week and is always packed with young people.

When the pastor approached the management of the club to see what it would take to rent the club out for the extra night to put on some meetings, the manager turned him down. But my pastor friend told him they would be willing to pay whatever price for it, so the manager told him he would rent it out for one night for $5,000. Deal done.

The way they ran the meetings was totally different than anything I had ever seen—totally non-religious with a live DJ that gave it the normal club feel as a huge dance party. The church had around 250 young people in their church, and they were asked to invite their unsaved Muslim friends to come to the meetings. The room was filled to capacity with around 700 young people. Some of them came off the streets drunk and expecting to step into the normal club that was usually full of drunk people dancing and partying. The live DJ played for a few hours. Late in the evening, they had some young people stand up to share some powerful testimonies of how God set them free and saved them.

At the very end of the night, they brought me up, and we began to move in words of knowledge and miracles. Deaf ears opened, tumors dissolved, and backs, legs, and eyes were healed. Over 20 people got healed right in the darkest nightclub in Jakarta, Indonesia. That night, over 80 Muslims gave their lives to Jesus.

This group in Indonesia has also conducted meetings in the Hard Rock Café in Jakarta when it's filled with unsaved Muslims, and have seen many come to know the Lord in that club as well.

Now is a time to get creative.

Light up the night.

Burn on.

Start Where You Are

Before I was ever in full-time ministry, God used me in sports. When I first got saved, I was playing baseball in college as well as semi pro. I saw God do all kinds of awesome things on the field. One time, while playing semi-pro baseball in Grand Junction, Colorado, I was pitching. In the second inning of the game, a batter fouled off a ball, and when he did, it deflected off of the bat and hit my catcher in his wrist, breaking it. The catcher fell on the ground, rolling all over the place at home plate, screaming. All of the coaches and umpires huddled around this guy to discuss what they should do. I heard one of them ask if they should call an ambulance. Then I heard the Lord speak to me and say, "I want you to go and pray for him to be healed right now."

So I walked up to home plate and asked my catcher if I could pray for him. As I did, the coaches and umpires looked at me with utter shock—as if I was crazy. I grabbed his wrist and prayed for him in front of a whole stadium of people and both teams. All I said to him was, "Be healed in Jesus' name." Then they took him off the field and put another catcher in. I ended up striking out the next two batters. Then, as I went into the dugout, something strange happened. The whole team was on one end of the dugout, and I noticed that I was left all alone on the other side. One of my teammates walked by me, cussed, looked at me, and said, "Oh sorry, man; I didn't mean to talk like that in front of you." It was as if everyone was suddenly afraid of me.

Two innings later, the catcher who had broken his wrist was declared totally healed, and they put him back in the game. He even got a hit, and we ended up winning the game. From that point on, I became respected at a new level on my team and began to see doors open to share with my teammates about

God. It was an amazing day, and all the fans in the stadium saw the glory of God.

God wants us to walk in dominion in the earth. Before my teammates saw that miracle, they were always cracking nasty jokes and cussing right in front of me. Some of them would do it on purpose, but something shifted as they saw the power of God released. All of a sudden, I began to be the one calling the shots as they stopped mocking God and the awe of God came upon all of them. If we will just be who we are called to be and not hide it, we will see awesome victories in the Lord, and He will cause us to become effective in our witnessing for His glory.

God wants to raise up professional athletes who will move in the supernatural and demonstrate God's glory in front of many. Now is the time to dream with God and reach the peaks of your sphere of influence. Become a dread champion and burn on.

Dream Big

We like to talk about examples of what it is to do big things for God and who is doing them, but I want to make something clear: I am by no means saying that unless you become a famous star or someone who is seen before the masses reaching large numbers of people that you are not doing big things for God and His Kingdom. What I am doing is highlighting people who have dreamed big for God and through Him are living out those dreams and making a difference in the world.

My prayer for those of you who read this book is that the testimonies will encourage you as well as spark faith in your hearts to believe God for more. The reality is God wants to use those who are seen in front of the masses as well as those who are living out everyday, ordinary lives. Everyone is different, and we all have unique callings and gifting. Not everyone is called to be a politician or rock star, but all of us are called to dream big with God and be used powerfully by Him in whatever sphere of influence He has given us. Some of the most powerful stories and testimonies I have ever heard often happen in the lives of those nobody knows. They are everyday, ordinary people who have an extraordinary God. So whether you are called to be a stay-at-home mom, a mechanic, or the next president of the United States of America, dream big for God and watch what God does.

Will you be one who will dream with God to do big things for His name's sake? Are you willing to allow God to shine through you to a lost and dying world and give you the gift of influence to reach them?

You need a bigger vision for life. God wants to take you from a place of false humility and being afraid of doing big things for Him and cause you to shine for His glory, to burn on in your daily life. He wants you to overcome the fear and religiosity that have crept into the Church. Religiosity tells you that dreaming big is a form of pride. The fear that you will not succeed or reach your dream is a tactic of the enemy. Neither is of God. But faith, trust, and love are.

In the Church today, we have sung worship songs that say things like, "Take the world and give me you" or "You're all I want and don't need anything else." These songs preach that we should practice a kind of false humility.

The devil came into society and released his influence to the world. God wants us to get it back. He wants us to stop running from the world as if they have some plague and begin to love them and show them the way. He wants His people to dream big with Him in this hour. If you have a real relationship with God, a relationship so deep that you know His voice, God will keep you from pride more quickly than the control of people ever could.

He wants you to start burning again with freedom and love and to burn on, a light shining for *all* to see.

> *Let your light shine before men in such a way that they may see your good works, and glorify your Father who is in Heaven* (Matthew 5:16 NASB).

Become a Burning One and burn on.

THE BURNING QUESTION

Take a look at your gifts and talents, the daydreams you have about being successful in one area of life, be it business, the arts, government, work, or ministry. Where do you see yourself standing three years from now? Five years from now? Tomorrow even? Can you see yourself on fire for God and releasing His presence there, in the midst of your work or artistic expression?

Your Response

_____

_____

_____

_____

_____

_____

_____

_____

_____

_____

_____

_____

_____

_____

_____

_____

_____

_____

A Prayer to Get You There

*Lord, You have created me for a purpose. I am
a dream come true from Your heart, birthed into
existence because of Your great love for me. I place
myself in Your hands so that You may direct me into
the divine appointments that You have scheduled for
me. Move me into the destiny You have called me
to. Release to me, even this week, a word of direction
and encouragement that will make me realize how
close You are to me and I am to You. Open up doors
of destiny and favor to me. I ask that You would
schedule a divine appointment for me in the coming
days and that You would set me up for success for
Your glory and honor. Thank You for taking every
opportunity to extend Your love and reveal it to
me in practical ways. Abba, I belong to You.
And You will never let me down.*

Endnote

1. Official minutes of the Indonesia Parliament
   (January 19, 2009), 25; http://translate.google.com/
   translate?hl=en&sl=id&u=http://www.dpr.go.id/
   archive/minutes/Risalah_Rapat_Paripurna_Ke-18_
   Masa_Sidang_III_Tahun_2008-2009.pdf&ei=oKKmTb
   7CMcLpgAey6IT0BQ&sa=X&oi=translate&ct=result
   &resnum=1&sqi=2&ved=0CBoQ7gEwAA&prev=/sea
   rch%3Fq%3DConstant%2BPonggawa%2BDPR%2BIsrae
   l%2B%28pdf%29%2BKASET%2B1%26hl%3Den%26pr
   md%3Divns; accessed April 19, 2011.

CHAPTER 6

PERSIST AND PURSUE

D read champions develop true faith—a faith that will scale the walls of injustice and take back what the enemy has stolen—a faith that is real enough to enable them to shake off their defeats—a faith that works in them so deeply that they persist until they have taken back what the enemy has stolen from them. Then they pursue the enemy until he repays seven times more than what he has stolen. God is going to raise up an army of champions who will not shrink back from the devil's attacks, but will actually gain momentum and strength from them. If the devil takes one out, 1,000 more will benefit from the justice of the attack.

They step into supernatural strength for the adventures and wars that they were called to. They become an army not just endowed with supernatural strength, but equipped by justice to win every skirmish set before them. No matter what battle you face or what mountain is staring back at you stirring up doubts and insecurities about your ability to climb, if your purpose is to release justice, you will win.

I had a dream one night in which God began to show me His plans to raise up an army of champions for His glory through the principles of justice.

In the dream, I was lying down in this huge room filled with about 20 bunk beds. The room had one big window in it, and the walls were made of cement. I knew that I was in an army barrack that housed the army of God. Soldiers were sleeping in their beds, resting for their next day of training. I could see the army fatigues and boots neatly folded at the foot of each bed. I knew in the dream that I was in a place where God was raising up an army for Himself. It was a place of equipping and training like when a natural army goes through a time of boot camp to prepare for war.

I noticed that everyone was asleep except for me, and beside every bunk bed there was a night table containing people's personal belongings. As I looked closely to the left of my bunk, I discovered a night table with a bunch of my personal stuff on it. I noticed three things on the table that belong to me—my wedding ring, my favorite watch, and my wallet. Then, just as I discovered this table with all of my personal belongings on it, I heard the sound of the one window in the room being forced open.

I watched as a man dressed all in black, with a black ski mask on covering his face, crawled through the window into the room. Then all of a sudden I realized that this man was a thief and he had broken into the room to steal from the sleeping men. The thief did not notice me watching him. So in the dream I acted like I was asleep. Then, as I pretended to be asleep, I watched as the man began to steal everyone's personal stuff, moving from night table to night table, robbing people's personal items and putting them into this big sack.

Then all of a sudden the man headed straight for my stuff, and as he did, I jumped out of my bed and wrestled the man to the ground. I put him in a headlock, and the man passed out. Then I noticed a phone that was in the room sitting on a table. I knew I needed to pick up the phone and report this thief to my authorities.

When I picked up the phone, the scene changed and I was no longer in the bunkroom with the other soldiers, but was now in a huge courtroom. I noticed a court case in progress. As I looked to the center of the room, I saw that Jesus was there. He was beautiful and dressed in judge's robes. I was amazed as I realized that I now stood before the righteous judge of all of Heaven and earth. Then I realized that I was a part of this great trial, and I also saw that the thief I had wrestled down was standing in the room.

Jesus looked intently at the thief and declared, "You were caught in the very act. Now sevenfold justice must be recompensed." Then Jesus slammed down the court hammer, and I watched as angels were sent immediately to bring His proclamation to pass. The dream ended with Jesus smiling at me as if I had won an amazing victory in God.

After I had the dream, I wrote it down, and the Lord began to speak to me about the experience over a period of about one year. At times I would close my eyes while in prayer about the meaning of the dream and the Holy Spirit would take me back into the experience and reveal to me different truths about how God is raising up an army for Himself who will become mighty champions for His glory and overcome the devil and his kingdom.

The first thing God began to speak to me about through this dream was how He was raising up an army for His glory that would manifest His love and Kingdom in the earth. He began to speak to me about how the Body of Christ was in a time and season of being equipped and trained for war. That's why I was in an army barrack in my dream.

Then He began to tell me that He was about to release new mantles of authority and power upon the Body of Christ for the purpose of an end-time harvest. He then said to me that the possessors of these mantles would be a generation who would walk in mighty demonstrations of His love and power like no other generation had before.

As He spoke this to me, I remembered the army fatigues and boots that were at the foot of the beds in my dream, neatly folded and ready to be put to use. Then the Lord said to me that those are the mantles that are to be given to those who are willing to wake up out of their slumber and fight the good fight of faith. After hearing all of this, I asked the Holy Spirit, "Where is all this at in the Bible? Where is there a connection between the army of God and His power?"

Then the Lord said, "*God's troops will willingly volunteer in the day of his power.*" (See Psalm 110:3.)

As the Holy Spirit highlighted this to me, I began to realize that now is not the time to be lukewarm and complacent, because God is about to awaken a generation to victory in the battle of light versus darkness. Then the Lord highlighted to me another verse:

> *Awake, awake! Put on your strength, O Zion; put on your beautiful garments, O Jerusalem, for the unclean and uncircumcised shall no longer come to you* (Isaiah 52:1).

He began to show me that there was an entire generation who would begin to walk victoriously over the devil and his kingdom through embracing the justice of God.

He began to speak to me about how He was going to use the attacks of the enemy or the thief to empower His people to become stronger in the Spirit than ever before. In fact, He showed me that they would not just overcome his attacks, but that they would become stronger and stronger every time the enemy would attack. His people needed to begin to understand the principles of God's justice. I remembered the thief in the dream and how he came through the window to steal people's personal stuff. Then I began to realize the importance of the words Jesus spoke to the thief. He said, "You have been caught in the very act. Let sevenfold justice be recompensed!"

I realized that I had heard these words before in the Word of God. In Scripture it says that when the thief is caught stealing from God's people, he must repay sevenfold what has been taken (see Prov. 6:30-31).

I knew that the Holy Spirit was giving me keys to overcome the enemy and his attacks as well as keys to step into being a part of His end-time army. I realized that every one of us Christians have been attacked by satan and his evil hordes at one time or another, and every one of us has been ripped off in some way or another by the powers of darkness in a personal way. As I was thinking about this, the Holy Spirit brought back to my memory the words of Jesus:

> *The thief does not come except to steal, and to kill, and to destroy. I have come that they may have life, and that they may have it more abundantly* (John 10:10).

As the Lord began to speak to me through this Scripture, I began to realize that Jesus came to the earth to take back what the enemy had stolen from His Father, as well as to restore to us as His people the right to live out an abundant life. He came that we might have eternal life as well as victory over the devil in every way! As I began to get this revelation, I realized that we are living in a time when, as the Body of Christ, we cannot afford to allow the enemy to beat us up and steal from us any longer.

It is time for God's people to begin to stand up and fight the good fight of faith and no longer allow the enemy to have the upper hand. So many Christians live way below the means the Father intended for them simply because they don't understand God's Word.

Psalm 97:1-6 lifts us to a higher way of thinking:

> *The LORD reigns; let the earth rejoice; let the multitude of isles be glad! Clouds and darkness surround Him; righteousness and justice are the foundation of His throne. A fire goes before Him, and burns up His enemies round about. His lightnings light the world; the earth sees and trembles. The mountains melt like wax at the presence of the LORD, at the presence of the Lord of the whole earth. The heavens declare His righteousness, and all the peoples see His glory.*

This Scripture shows us that the very foundations of God's throne are righteousness and justice. It shows us that God longs to declare His nature and goodness over His enemies.

One of the key ways God displays His rule and reign is through the justice of God. God never intended that we as Christians would live out defeated lives, being oppressed by the devil, with no hope for a future or destiny. Jesus intended that we would live out an abundant life in which we would obtain peace, joy, and righteousness that would cause us to have victory over the enemy at all times.

If we are to live out this abundant life, we have to understand the justice of God, and we have to understand our rights as sons and daughters of God. The enemy can't just run around doing whatever he pleases. He can only do what he has a legal right to do in the spirit. That, however, does not stop him from overstepping his boundaries. Like I said earlier, the devil is a thief who comes to steal, kill, and destroy. He shows up at times when we least expect it, but we don't have to let him get away with it. What we need to do is learn how to deal with the enemy when he rears his head up and attacks. Just like in my dream, we need to catch the thief in the very act of his attacks and call out to our authorities, which would be God the Father and the righteous judge Jesus Christ.

In my dream, the enemy came when all were asleep and began to steal people's stuff. Then I jumped on him and ended up receiving Heaven's help as I called on my authorities from earth. God wants us to be victorious over the devil. Just like in the laws of the natural world and land, we have a right to claim justice in a court of law against those who have wronged us. We also have the right to receive justice from a court and system that's not of this earth.

The key to receiving God's justice is catching the thief in the act of his attack or recognizing when we have been illegally attacked and then asking or crying out to God for justice for what our adversary has done to us. If we cry out, He will answer. We need to become like the persistent widow who cried out to the unrighteous judge for justice and would not stop until he gave it to her.

PERSIST UNTIL JUSTICE IS RELEASED

Let's look at that parable.

Then He spoke a parable to them, that men always ought to pray and not lose heart, saying: "There was in a certain city a judge who did not fear God nor regard man.

Now there was a widow in that city; and she came to him, saying, 'Get justice for me from my adversary.'

And he would not for a while; but afterward he said within himself, 'Though I do not fear God nor regard man, yet because this widow troubles me I will avenge her, lest by her continual coming she weary me.'"

Then the Lord said, "Hear what the unjust judge said. And shall God not avenge His own elect who cry out day and night to Him, though He bears long with them? I tell you that He will avenge them speedily. Nevertheless, when the Son of Man comes, will He really find faith on the earth?" (Luke 18:1-8)

In this story, Jesus admonishes us to not give up when things get hard, but to continue praying even when things don't seem to go right and we seem to be under attack by the enemy. It's easy to pray a couple of times and then give up, but Jesus wants us to understand the persistent heart of the widow found in this parable. She did not relent from asking the unjust judge for justice. She eventually received it because of her continual asking. She asked so much that the unjust judge said to himself that he must give her justice *"lest she weary me."*

Then, Jesus went on to say that if the unjust judge would listen to the woman's cry, how much more would the Father in Heaven listen to His own sons and daughters and speedily avenge them?

It's all about perspective.

God wants us to understand that if persistence worked in changing the unjust judge's heart, how much more will it move the heart of the Father in Heaven who loves His sons and daughters! Jesus even goes on to say that the Father longs to speedily avenge His own people as they cry out.

Sometimes we stop praying just short of a breakthrough.

> *Ask, and it will be given to you; seek, and you will find; knock, and it will be opened to you. For everyone who asks receives, and he who seeks finds, and to him who knocks it will be opened* (Matthew 7:7-8).

True faith has action behind it. It believes when we can't see and keeps going until God answers. That's why, at the end of the story of the persistent widow, Jesus says in Luke 18:8, "*When the Son of Man comes, will He really find faith on the earth?*" God wants us to be persistent in prayer and to not lose heart when we don't see the answer right away.

Daniel is a great example of persistence in prayer. In Daniel 10, we discover that he cried out day and night and even fasted for 21 days until he finally got a breakthrough. The breakthrough came when the angel of the Lord appeared to him and told him that the Lord had answered his prayer the very hour it was asked, but that the prince of Persia stood against him to oppose the answer from coming.

Sometimes the reason our prayers don't instantly get answered is because warfare comes against our prayers in the spirit. Ephesians 6:12 talks about this warfare:

> For we do not wrestle against flesh and blood, but against principalities, against powers, against the rulers of the darkness of this age, against spiritual hosts of wickedness in the heavenly places.

We must walk in persistence like Daniel did in prayer. If we will continually knock, seek, and ask, we will see our prayers answered. What would have happened if Daniel had given up on day 10 or even 20? We have to recognize our authority and rights as sons and daughters and ask God for the victory. We have to always keep in our hearts and minds the fact that the Father is good and wants to do good for His sons and daughters.

There is power in prayer, and it is a weapon that God has given us to overcome the devil. We see this in Second Corinthians 10:3-4:

> For though we walk in the flesh, we do not war according to the flesh. For the weapons of our warfare are not carnal but mighty in God for pulling down strongholds.

What we need to do is become like the persistent widow and recognize when we have been done wrong by our adversary the devil and continually cry for breakthrough until God answers.

Now let's look at another aspect of my justice dream that pertains to what to ask God justice for. God wants us to recognize when we have had things stolen from us and then make a demand on Heaven to move in justice; it forces the hand of the enemy to restore what he took—sevenfold.

Pursue Until Restoration Happens

As I thought about the three items the enemy had tried to take, the Lord began to speak to me about each one. He began to tell me that each item had a symbolic meaning that pertained to an aspect of justice that He wanted to begin to release to His people.

The Ring

First He began to speak to me about the ring. In the natural, the ring that was in my dream on the night table was my wedding ring. He began to tell me that the ring was a sign of covenant and had to do with relationships and that it was His desire to begin to restore things to the Body in the area of relationships.

He then said, "Jerame, I want to begin to restore relationships the devil has stolen from My people. I want to restore back to My people who have suffered loss of friends and family for the Gospel's sake."

As He said this, I thought about lost relationships with friends and family members that I had suffered since giving my life to Jesus. The Holy Spirit began to remind me of Mark 10:29-30:

> ... There is no one who has left house or brothers or sisters or father or mother or wife or children or lands, for My sake and the Gospel's, who shall not receive a hundredfold now in this time—houses and brothers and sisters and mothers and children and lands, with persecutions—and in the age to come, eternal life.

God wants to give us justice in every area of our lives, especially in the area of relationships.

God wants Heaven to invade earth, and He wants circumstances to change in our lives regarding relationships, and the best part is that He wants us to receive recompense and blessing now. He said that we would receive a hundredfold in this lifetime, not one day far off in the future when we die and go to Heaven.

It's time that we begin to cry out to the righteous judge and ask for sevenfold justice, and even a hundredfold justice, in the area of relationships, family, and friends that we have lost. Since the Lord began to show me that He wanted to restore relationships to His people, I began to make a demand on Heaven for my non-Christian family members and friends whom I lost relationship with when I got saved. Then all of a sudden, childhood friends began to contact me and ask me about God. It was amazing how quickly it began to happen. I had no contact with some of the individuals for years.

Justice in relationships can mean that those we know personally return to us and to the Lord. But sevenfold or hundredfold justice means that many more come along for the ride. One of the things we have gone after in our ministry over the years is souls. We have seen many decisions for Christ over the last five years, and one of the ways we have tapped into seeing so many saved is that we began to ask the Lord for sevenfold justice in the area of friends and family members we have lost who never came to know the Lord. We began to make a demand on God to release to us a soul-winning anointing as well as open doors to preach the Gospel and see people get saved. Since discovering God's heart for justice and crying out for it in the area of souls, we have been to over 27 nations and seen over 30,000 decisions for Christ.

God does not want us to live defeated; He wants us to be victorious in all that we do.

You may have suffered the loss of family members or friends, not just due to your faith, but sickness or disease. One of the hardest things to experience and overcome as a Christian is a family member or friend dying from sickness or disease. Your faith takes a hard hit during times like this—unless you understand the power of God's love and justice. God wants to give you justice. He wants you to tap into His heart and overcome the attacks of the devil. One of the strongest attacks against the Body of Christ is sickness and disease.

Many Christians who once lived in faith have had their faith in God rocked because of the loss of a family member. Many even lose faith in the supernatural power of God and His love and have bought into the lies of the enemy—lies that God does not really love them or that God is not really good. God wants to redeem His name and give to His people sevenfold justice in the area of death in the Body of Christ.

There are far too many Christians who are dying yearly from sicknesses and diseases like cancer and other life-threatening conditions. We must put an end to these attacks of the enemy. Jesus said in Luke 10:19 that He has given us authority to trample on serpents and scorpions and over all the power of the enemy and that nothing shall by any means hurt us. When this sort of thing happens to us, we face one of two choices. The first is that we can buy into the plan of the enemy and doubt the goodness and love of God's nature and character. Along the way, we lose all faith in the supernatural power of God to save, heal, and deliver. Or we can take on the second choice and realize that sickness and disease are an attack from the devil and not something given from God to teach someone a lesson.

The key is to understand that the devil came to steal, kill, and destroy; Jesus came that we might have life and life abundantly.

This Scripture shows us that the devil will steal or trespass in our lives if we let him, and there are times when he clearly crosses the line. When this happens, we need to stand up and fight. We should not have a victim mentality and give up, but recognize that God is always good, and He never changes. He is on our side, and His goodness and love will not be mocked by the enemy.

Several years ago, my grandmother was diagnosed with terminal lymphoma breast cancer. She fought it for a long time and underwent chemotherapy. Then the cancer multiplied in the form of cancerous tumors, eventually spreading throughout her whole body until she passed away. She died at only 67 years old. It was clearly premature. My family was devastated. My grandmother was like the glue that held our entire extended family together on my mom's side. Here we were, praying for her to get healed, and the miracle never manifested.

I remember the temptation to be angry with God and upset that she didn't get her miracle and to begin to doubt in His existence. But instead of allowing those feelings and temptations to get the best of me, I stirred up my faith. I just chose to believe that God is good, even if I didn't understand why my grandmother was not healed.

A few years later, as I began to learn about the justice of God, I started making a demand on God for the death of my grandmother.

So I said to God, "Lord, I want justice for this attack against my family and against my grandmother. I'm asking for sevenfold what was stolen from me. In fact, God, I want a sevenfold anointing to destroy sickness and disease and especially cancer and tumors."

I made my demand to God specific and grounded it in Proverbs 6:30-31:

> People do not despise a thief if he steals to satisfy himself when he is starving. Yet when he is found, he must restore sevenfold; he may have to give up all the substance of his house.

Since that day I pulled on Heaven and made a demand on the Scripture, declaring the power of His Word and promise, one of the miracles we have seen the most is people healed from terminal cancer and tumors. In fact, we have seen over 20 cases of cancer healed since the beginning of our ministry. We have tapped into the justice of God. To some it may have looked like the devil won when my grandmother died, but really her life became a seed that went into the ground to bring life to many.

One night in Concord, North Carolina, we were speaking at a meeting with about 1,000 people attending. During the worship, I went into an open vision where the Lord began to open my eyes to see what He intended to do that night in the miraculous. In the vision, I could see on the right side of the room five people with tumors and four others over on the left side. I watched as the fire of God burned them up. After the vision, I asked the Lord what the vision meant, and He told me that there were five women on the right side of the room with tumors or cysts on their breasts and four women on the left side of the room with the same condition. He told me to call them out and pray for them on the stage.

So at the beginning of the meeting, just after they called me up to speak, I told the crowd my vision. I said, "If that's you, come up to the stage right now. God is going to heal you."

Exactly five came from the right and four women from the left. Then, as I laid my hands on their heads, one by one they began to be healed. Another woman saw them getting healed, and she couldn't resist. She ran up to the stage to receive healing.

After we prayed, we asked the ladies to check privately to see if they were healed. One by one, they came back and gave testimonies that God had healed them. All ten women were healed that night from the tumors and cysts in the breast. God did exactly what He showed me—and more. He showed me nine women with this condition, and He went above and beyond and did ten. God is so good!

After the meeting ended, I thought about the miracles that had taken place, and the Lord reminded me of my prayer for justice because of the death of my grandmother regarding cancer and tumors. It was then that I realized that God's goodness will always prevail over the attacks of the thief, and His justice will come through without fail.

Are you one who has lost a loved one prematurely to sickness and disease? Or are you one who has suffered the loss of your faith from an attack against a loved one who died? If so, it's time to make a demand on the justice of God and ask the Lord Jesus for a sevenfold anointing to destroy sickness and disease. Ask Him for opportunities to pray for those hurting with sickness and disease and see them healed. Remember, be specific and make a demand on God for sevenfold justice.

If your faith has been shaken by the loss of a loved one or your trust in God's love has been hindered, then ask God for justice in those areas. Ask Him for sevenfold the faith and trust you lost, and watch as the Lord releases a radical gift of faith and trust that you never had before. God is good!

Let's look at some other areas I believe that God wants to bring justice to.

PLACE A DEMAND ON GOD AND REDEEM THE TIME

The second item on the night table that the thief tried to steal was my watch. After praying into the meaning of the watch, the Lord began to speak to me about His desire to restore time that the devil had stolen from people.

As He spoke this to me, I began to think about how so many people I knew felt like the devil had stolen time from them and that they had missed their calling. I began to think about how even in my own life when I first came to know the Lord I felt like the devil stole some of the best years of my youth. I didn't get saved until I was 22 years old, and I spent most of my younger days just getting drunk, doing drugs, and being caught up in worldly living. After I met the Lord, I felt like I had really wasted away a lot of my life with carnal living. I thought if I could have just served the Lord in my younger years, the years would have been more awesome than what I experienced. I could have traveled the nations preaching the Gospel to the poor and walked out the Great Commission, seeing souls won for Jesus. Then, about a year into being saved, I began to press into God and started developing a friendship with Him, and all of the guilt and shame of the past that I thought I had lost went away.

In the meanwhile, I kind of felt like the prodigal son Jesus talked about who had wasted away his life with prodigal living (see Luke 15:11-31).

The Lord began to speak to me about time from God's point of view. God does not look at time the same way we do. In His Word, it says that *"With the Lord one day is as a thousand years, and a thousand years is as one day"* (2 Pet. 3:8). God can make up time where we may feel like it has slipped away. What seems like an eternity for us could only be a moment of time in the eyes of the Lord.

It is nothing for God to make up lost time. God wants to take those who have felt like they have wasted their past and not accomplished much in life and anoint them with a spirit of acceleration and joy. Like He did with the prodigal son, He wants to place His robes of righteousness upon our lives, as well as give us a signet ring of sonship and place the sandals of the

Gospel of peace upon our feet. He even wants to kill the fatted cow and have a big party in celebration that the old is gone and the new has come! God wants us to look forward to what is ahead and not at what is behind us.

God wants us to place a demand on His Word and make a claim to regain the time that was stolen.

I began to make a demand on time that I felt was stolen from me. Shortly after I did, a spirit of acceleration came upon my life, and I was launched into full-time ministry—after only being saved for four years. Since that time, we have been in over 27 nations preaching the Gospel of the Kingdom, seeing thousands come to know the Lord. God made up for the time I felt I had lost because of my past mistakes.

No matter where you came from or what you have done or how much time you think you have lost, God is able to make up for it. Jesus wants you to know that your best days are ahead of you and not behind. Just like it says in Haggai 2:9, "'*The glory of this latter temple shall be greater than the former,*' says the LORD *of hosts. 'And Iin this place I will give peace,*' says the LORD *of hosts.*" God wants to give you peace if you think that time has slipped away from you. He wants the latter part of your life to be awesome!

This goes for people of all ages. Even if you are 70 years old, your better days can be ahead of you if you choose to believe and ask for sevenfold justice. So if you are one who feels that the devil has stolen time from you, cry out to God for justice in this area. Ask Him to accelerate things in your life and begin to make up for the time the thief has stolen, and watch what happens.

RESTORING THE FAVOR OF GOD

The last thing on my nightstand was my wallet. As I prayed about the wallet, the Lord began to show me that my wallet represented the favor and finances of God as well as our identity in Christ. He then began to tell me that one of the areas He wanted to begin to give justice to the Body of Christ in was the area of finances and favor. He said, "Jerame, I want to begin to restore to My people finances, lands, property, and areas of business that went wrong because of the attacks of the devil."

God wants to restore to His people sevenfold in every area of attack against their wallet or finances. If you were ripped off by the thief, you need to make your claim in the courts of Heaven.

I believe the wallet is metaphorical for several things. In your wallet you can find all kinds of different stuff—like money, IDs, credit cards, and well, all sorts of personal stuff. I believe that all of these things are significant for what God is about to release— justice to the Body of Christ.

First let's talk about our ID cards and credit cards. These two things represent our identities in Christ and our credibility with people. They speak about the favor of God upon our lives. God wants to restore identity and credibility with people who have experienced the pain of others who have talked falsely behind their backs and damaged their reputation. Some have had people tell lies about them or gossip behind their backs. As a result, they may have lost favor in relationships or jobs or even a sense of who they are in the Lord for a season.

God wants to bring justice to relationships. He is the God who gives us favor with Him as well as other people. The Bible says that Jesus *"increased in favor with God and men"* (Luke 2:52). This shows us that God knows that we, too, need favor, and He will give us increased favor with people.

If any of these things apply to you, it's time to call upon the righteous judge of the earth who sees all and knows all to release to you sevenfold justice for what the enemy has done to you.

One of the other areas that God wants to release justice to His people in is in the area of finances. This was the first thing I thought about when I prayed about the meaning of the wallet. Many have been ripped off financially through loss of a job or someone stealing from them. Now is the time to ask God for justice. I believe that we are living in a time when, as the people of God, we must begin to recognize that God is our provider and not people, and even though the economic systems of this world may shake, we are not under the world's system anymore. We are under God's economic system, and we live by His provision and what the Word of God says.

God's Word tells us that our Father owns the cattle on a thousand hills and that it's His will that we would be the lenders and not the borrowers and the head and not the tail (see Ps. 50:10; Deut. 28:12-13). We are living in a time when God is going to release justice for the hits that we have taken because of the world system we live in.

A few years ago God began to speak to me about the finances of Heaven. It happened while on a missions trip to Indonesia and Singapore. As my contact from Singapore dropped me off to send me to the airport, he handed me a financial seed of blessing. He sowed 350 Singaporean dollars into me. As I got to the airport, I realized that I needed to get a gift for my brother's wedding, as I was going to be the best man a week after I returned to America. We checked our bags in at the airport, went through security, and started looking for a gift in the Singapore airport. I found a guys-n-girls set of watches that I really liked and thought about buying them as a gift. The price of the watches was around 500 Singaporean dollars. As I was looking at the watches, my friend told me he was hungry, so I told the man working at the shop I would think about it, and if I wanted to get the watches, I would come back later.

We went to eat some sushi, and after we did, I decided to get the watches. While at dinner, I explained to my friend that I wanted to get the watches and that I would have to use some U.S. cash to pay for the watches, along with the $350 that my contact had given me. So we went back down to the watch shop and I told the guy working there I would take them. So he took them out and rang them up, and they came up to 497.64 Singaporean dollars. I took out my 350 Singaporean dollars and started to count them out to give to the store clerk. As I did, I was surprised to find that I now had 400 Singaporean dollars in my hands, so I told my friend, "I think my money just multiplied. Just a minute ago I only had 350 dollars, and now I have 400."

Then my friend said to me, "Count it again." So I did and was shocked as the money multiplied again and went from 400 to 450. Then the store clerk who was watching this miracle happen as well said, "Count it again." So I counted it a third time and it multiplied to 500 Singaporean dollars right in front of all three of us.

It was amazing. The money started multiplying right there as I was counting it. I started off with 350 dollars that I had counted many times, and it multiplied to 500, and I was able to buy the watches for my brother's wedding without having to use any of my own cash.

On my plane ride home from Singapore to LA, God spoke to me about this whole miracle. He said to me, "Jerame, don't you want to know what the sign of the multiplication of the finances means?"

Then I said, "Yes, Lord."

He replied, "You were buying watches for a bride and groom for a wedding, and I want you to tell my people this. It's a new time and a new season when the Bridegroom from Heaven is going to supernaturally provide for His bride on the earth to do all that she is called to do. Tell them that in this next season, I am going to provide for My people, and they must learn to trust Me."

As God spoke this to me, I was excited and realized that this sign of the money was much more than just a miracle. It was a message from God to me and His people. After this happened, I asked Him where this all was in His Word. I said, "Show me where You promised to supernaturally provide for all that Your people are called to do."

The Holy Ghost led me to Second Corinthians 9:8:

> *And God is able to make all grace abound toward you, that you, always having all sufficiency in all things, may have an abundance for every good work.*

As God spoke this to me, I began to see that it was God's will to provide for us, and not only was it His will, but He also wanted to do it. As a Bridegroom from Heaven, He wants to release supernatural intervention on behalf of His bride and cause her to tap into all that she needs to do the things that God has called her to do.

If you are in a place where the enemy has stolen from you financially or you have lost favor or reputation, now is your time to call upon the righteous judge of Heaven and earth to release to you justice. Don't allow bitterness to get into your heart and steal your provision. It's time to realize that the enemy wants to stop you from entering into your destiny. He wants to stop you from tapping into Heaven's supply over your life so that you never do what you are called to do in life. Forgive those whom the devil has used as pawns in the chess game he plays against your life, and ask justice from your Bridegroom in Heaven who is the righteous judge, and watch Him avenge His people with sevenfold repayment.

God wants to restore to His people sevenfold in every area of attack against their wallet or finances. If you were ripped off by the thief, you need to make your claim in the courts of Heaven. There are some in the Body who have been involved in business projects that went sideways. God wants to give you back what has been taken from you. It's time to begin to cry out to God to restore what has been taken from you and ask for greater opportunities to come your way.

Now is a time of advancement. While the world is under the curse of the world system, you are not. You are under the blessings and favor of your Father in Heaven, and it's time to recognize it. Take some time to spend with the Lord, and allow Him to show you the areas in your life were He wants to give you justice, and begin to make decrees and prayers to the Lord for sevenfold what has been stolen from you.

The Burning Question

Can you identify three things that the enemy has stolen from you? Is it finances? A relationship? Your identity? How badly do you want them back? Can you feel a righteous anger stirring in you enough to ask God to make the enemy repay sevenfold what he has taken? You may not get the relationship restored, but you can ask for another one or for a ministry of reconciliation that will enable you to see hundreds of relationships restored in the power and love of Christ. You may not receive that inheritance that was stolen from you by a relative, but you may receive sevenfold the amount through another means. Ask big! Expect more.

Your Response

_____

_____

_____

_____

_____

_____

_____

_____

_____

_____

_____

_____

_____

_____

_____

_____

_____

A Prayer to Get You There

Lord, I ask that You would move on my behalf to call the enemy to restore what he has stolen from me—and more. I place a demand on the Word that calls for justice. Release Your justice to me in the areas of _____. I thank You and praise You that You back up Your Word and You will bring it swiftly to pass. Let me be one who releases the justice of God to others. Commission me into Your plans and purposes for me as a dread champion who releases the justice of God in the very areas where the enemy has sought to rob, kill, and destroy me and my family. Here I am, Lord! Send Me!

CHAPTER 7

STRANGE FIRE

If you are going to burn with the fire of God and become a dread champion, you will need to become so close to the Holy Spirit that you will be able to discern the difference between true fire and strange fire. You will need to realize that who you are is God's most loved son or daughter. And who you are becoming is someone the world is about to take notice of—a child of the most High King—one who is destined to rule and reign with Him in the high places of society's influence as politicians, athletes, artists, prophets, and apostles in unlikely places—and in the low places of the streets. Where are you headed? What kind of a leader do you want to be known as?

Not long ago, while ministering in the Dudley outpouring in England, I realized what God wants to do in you and through you and into the region in which you live. I saw it in Lakeland, Florida, as well as many places where we have been. And we will see it again and again.

One night, Trevor Baker, pastor of a church called Revival Fires in Dudley, England, stood up and began to read and talk about a prophetic word that Smith Wigglesworth gave over the UK before he died. Trevor talked about how Smith prophesied that in the last days God was going to release a mighty outpouring of God's Spirit that would take place in the UK and all over the world. In this prophecy, Smith said that the greatest revival or outpouring that the UK had ever seen would happen when the Spirit and the Word would work together, hand to hand. When I heard that, it made my heart jump because the Lord spoke to me before I went to the UK and said, "I am sending you as a voice to England, to demonstrate the Spirit's power and to bring the Word of the Lord as well." We are going to see the Word of God and the Spirit of God burning through the land.

I believe that we are in a day when we are starting to see "first fruit" fires of what God is going to do. All over the world, God is sparking different moves and outpourings like the ones known as the Toronto Blessing, the Florida Outpouring, the Dudley Outpouring, and even the Bay of the Holy Spirit Revival recently launched in Alabama. I believe that these moves of God are first fruit fires of what God wants to do.

Get ready for God to begin to blow your mind! I don't believe that we have seen anything yet. God is about to release notable, remarkable miracles all over the world. When this move of His Spirit begins, it's not just going to be through the preachers and in churches that God is going to move. It's going to happen through everybody, and it will be a move of God that will spill into the streets. God's fire is going to pour into the streets and keep on spreading.

His winds will blow upon the fire sparked by a Burning One and spread it through the community, into the region, and sometimes, throughout the nation. We have to understand what God's doing and why it's happening so we can walk in the Spirit and see the fullness of God come rather than flame out or unintentionally morph it into some strange fire that will eventually burn out. We need to understand the purpose for why God releases outpourings of God. That way, when He does release them, we don't get sidetracked.

Read on.

I remember preaching in Lakeland, Florida, during the time when a revival burned through GodTV to the world known as the Florida Outpouring. It was an amazing time and such a privilege to be able to minister in that outpouring. As I ministered in one of the night meetings, miracles happened like crazy. The atmosphere was charged with the presence of God among more than 7,000 people who were full of faith and expectancy. As I ministered that night, the power of God's Spirit fell, and many notable and remarkable signs and wonders broke out everywhere.

After praying over the crowd for God's release of healing at the beginning of the meeting, we received testimonies of what God did. The first guy we interviewed said that as we released the healing wave of God's power, God recreated his blind eye. Apparently, when he was 1 year old, someone threw a rock at him and hit him in the eye, totally blinding him. The second testimony was from a woman who said that God had dissolved a metal rod that had been in her back for years due to a car accident. The third miracle involved a boy and his mother who testified that her son had been born deaf and could now hear.

We interviewed over 60 people that night who testified to receiving instantaneous miracles from God in their bodies. As awesome as all of these miracles were, the thing that touched my heart the most was all of the souls who were being won to Jesus, day in and day out. The miracles and the salvations didn't just stop with the speakers and the church services. It spilled out into the streets of Lakeland, and thousands were being saved.

I remember one of the other times I preached in Lakeland in a morning session. That day, God put it in my heart to speak on evangelism and to equip and train people to take the same power that was happening in the outpouring meetings to the streets. I ended up preaching a message on evangelism and going after the lost and bringing in the harvest. Then my wife, Miranda, and I laid hands on everyone for impartation and sent them out. That day, over 350 people got saved in the streets. Within three days, over 500 were saved in the streets. That same day that we released the impartation, a man gave a testimony in the night meeting of how he and his friends won 138 souls in one day. As I saw this happening, I knew that the Florida Outpouring was a real deal move of God. It was an authentic move defined by people who were being saved, healed, and delivered every night and every day as it spilled out of the meetings and into the streets.

I believe that the whole purpose of an outpouring from God's perspective is to revive His Church and bring souls into the Kingdom. People can say what they want about the Florida Outpouring, but I believe it was a first fruit fire of what God is going to do in the days to come. The Florida Outpouring was not so much about Todd Bentley or a man, although God used Todd to spark this great revival. We need to recognize the importance of what God was doing in the Spirit and stop focusing on the failures of a man.

If we put all of our hope and trust in people, we will always be disappointed, but if we put our hope and trust in God, He will never disappoint. The greatest thing we can do in situations like the Florida Outpouring is learn from them. We have to learn from the past mistakes of those who have gone on before us so that we don't make the same mistakes in the future. The reality is that God is pouring out His Spirit, and there will be more outpourings to come in the near future all around the world.

God is going to release outpourings of His Spirit that won't flow through just one leader or a small group of people. They will be released worldwide and through many leaders. The reason why I say this is because the idea of outpourings are a principle in God's Word and not some buzzword that people have come up with to attract people to themselves. Acts 2:17-19 says that God is going to pour out His Spirit on all flesh, that His sons and daughters are going to prophesy, that God's people are going to see signs and wonders in the heavens above and in the earth beneath, and that all who call upon the name of the Lord will be saved. The days of just the one-person show are over. There is a new breed of Christianity rising, and it will be a move of fathers and mothers and sons and daughters.

God wants to change the way we think, and He wants to move us out of the four walls of the church to begin to partner with Him to pour out His Spirit on all flesh. God wants us to know that the purpose for outpourings is this—so we can bring in a harvest of souls for Him. God the Father is raising up Burning Ones who will burn to bring the Lamb of God the reward for His sufferings.

Take the Land

Now let's take a deeper look at this idea of outpourings and God pouring out His Spirit on all flesh. I want to bring some definition to what an outpouring really is. In the Body of Christ, we like to use what I term as buzzwords. Buzzwords are popular sayings or phrases that we come up with that sound good to the ears. Some like to use buzzwords to attract the attention of people so they will show up to their events or get people excited for something they don't really understand.

For the past few years, it seems like everywhere I have been going and ministering, I have been hearing people talking or preaching about "Outpourings of God's Spirit." Everywhere I go, people even sing songs about outpourings and ask God to open the flood gates of Heaven and allow the rains of His Spirit to fall, but I don't know if people truly understand what they are asking God for. I'm not fully convinced that anyone even knows what an outpouring is. What are the rains of God's Spirit, and what does an outpouring of God look like? I believe God wants to give us more understanding of what outpourings are and what they look like so that, as Burning Ones, we can begin to position ourselves to receive all we need from God to take entire cities, regions, and nations.

In order for us to understand what a true outpouring of God looks like, we must look to the Word of God. God gave Moses what I call the precepts or conditions to entering into the land of promise or revival, a land overflowing with milk and honey.

> *For the land which you go to possess is not like the land of Egypt from which you have come, where you sowed your seed and watered it by foot, as a vegetable garden; but the land which you cross over to possess is a land of hills and valleys, which drinks water from the rain of Heaven, a land for which the LORD your God cares; the eyes of the LORD your God are always on it, from the beginning of the year to the very end of the year. And it shall be that if you will earnestly obey My commandments which I command you today, to love the LORD your God and serve Him with all your heart and with all your soul, then I will give you the rain for your land in its season, the early rain and the latter rain, that you may gather in your grain, your new wine, and your oil* (Deuteronomy 11:10-14).

The land of promise, which Moses and the people of God were to possess, would be a land that was dependent upon the rains of Heaven in order to receive a harvest. This is one of the most important aspects of an outpouring. God wants us to understand that the reason why He wants to pour out His Spirit on all flesh is so that harvest can happen. True signs of an outpouring include people being revived as well as saved. This is one of the reasons why God wants to raise up Burning Ones—so they can burn brightly with the fire of God, refreshing others as well as bringing in a massive harvest of souls at the end of the age.

In verse 14, it says that God pours out the rains of Heaven so that the people of God can gather in the harvest. Notice what the harvest looks like in this Scripture. It's defined as grain, new wine, and oil. These are the three basic provisions that He promised His people would receive as they entered into the land of promise. The grain represents the prophetic word of God coming to pass. The new wine represents the joy of the Lord, which is our strength. And the oil is symbolic for the fire of the Holy Ghost or the anointing. These three things always show up when God pours out His Spirit.

We also find all three of these things showing up on the Day of Pentecost. As Jesus rose from the dead and sat down at the right hand of the Father, the oil of God appeared upon the 120 disciples who were praying in the upper room, releasing tongues of fire upon their heads. Then, the new wine or joy of the Lord showed up, causing them to speak with other tongues, and the people of their day thought they were drunk on wine (see Acts 2:1-13). The grain of God also manifested as Peter stood up on that day and preached Jesus as the Christ, and all who heard the word that day were cut to the heart, and around 3,000 were saved as the prophetic promise of God's Word began to be fulfilled right in front of their eyes (see Acts 2:14-41). These three things will enter our lives as we begin to tap into the promises of God. They are what will bring us victory over the giants in the land and cause us to be triumphant over the enemy, seeing many brought out of his kingdom and into the Kingdom of God.

Now that we know what the purpose of the rains of Heaven are for, let's look at how to position ourselves as dread champions to receive and release the rains of God.

The second thing I want to point out about the passage above is that the revivals that God is going to be torching off in the near future are not going to look like the revivals in the past. God told Moses that he was going to possess a land that would be different than the land that he and the Hebrew children had come out of.

> For the land which you go to possess is not like the land of Egypt from which you have come, where you sowed your seed and watered it by foot, as a vegetable garden; but the land which you cross over to possess is a land of hills and valleys, which drinks water from the rain of Heaven (Deuteronomy 11:10-11).

Now look what God told Moses—an old guy doing a new thing. Isn't that kind of a funny thing to think about—a garden *watered by foot, as a vegetable garden?* How can you water your garden by foot? I'll tell you what it means. If you are to understand a lot of things in the Bible, you will need to understand them from a Hebrew mindset or point of view. The Bible was not written from a Western mindset, but a Hebrew context. In order to understand this passage and what it is saying, you have to understand the context of the point of view from the time and day it was written from.

This whole part of Scripture is all about receiving a harvest from God. It is all about receiving the grain, the oil, and the new wine. What God is doing in this part of the Scriptures is challenging Moses and the Hebrew children to change the way they thought about receiving a harvest or revival from God. He was showing them that as they moved forward into the Promised Land of God, the way they received a harvest had to change because it would no longer depend on watering gardens by foot, but would depend upon the rains of Heaven.

The reason why this language of watering gardens by foot is mentioned is because it rains very little in Egypt. The main source of water in the land of Egypt is the Nile River. Since there's no rain in Egypt, they would dig trenches by foot in the sand and plant the seeds in the trenches. Then they would use a device called a "shut-it," which was a long pole with a bucket on the end of it. They would then dip this pole into the Nile River, and wherever they had dug their trenches by foot, they would simply kick the pole over with their foot and control the water by hand; thus it would run right down the trenches they had prepared. That is how they watered the seed in a vegetable garden by foot. That was how they did it when they were in Egypt—the land of their bondage.

What God was saying to Moses in this Scripture was that things were going to be different as they entered into the land of promise regarding their ability to receive provision from Him. He was showing them that no longer would their provision or harvest be dependent upon themselves or their own efforts and control, but that it would be dependent upon the rains of Heaven, which meant God, Himself, would do it.

The first thing God wants us to understand about receiving an outpouring of His Spirit is that we have to take our hands off the "shut-it" and allow Him to have His way. We must stop digging our own trenches through human-made attempts to produce revival through programs and methodologies, and we must start to be dependent upon God's Spirit to do it. The second thing is that we have to let go of trying to control God's Spirit. Who can control an outpouring of rain in the natural besides God? God wants His people to no longer control how much water or rain He can release.

Some churches today only want a little bit of God, but not the fullness of who He is. They only want a little water here and a little water there and essentially are acting like the Hebrew children by trying to control how much water is released into the trenches. God is raising up Burning Ones who are going to walk in great discernment when it comes to the things of the Spirit. They will be those who will love the Lord their God with all of their hearts and be sensitive to God's voice and won't try to make revival a method or a form. They will flow out of a place of intimacy and obedience to God's Word and voice, and outpourings of God's Spirit will follow them everywhere they go, producing harvests of souls for the Kingdom of God.

Look who is taking the land: not the wise or the educated, not the rich and the famous, but those who are fully committed to Him—the Burning Ones, the dread champions. They are bold as lions, roaring with authority that makes unbelievers tremble under the glory of God and sometimes even look a little drunk. God's presence has a strange impact on people during times of revival.

I remember when the Lord first began to teach me about His presence. I was doing evangelism in Vancouver, BC, hanging out with some interns, and the Lord spoke to me about going outside of Starbucks immediately. We went outside of Starbucks and hung out and waited. About a half hour went by, and I thought, *Well, I guess I missed it.* Next thing I know, a guy rolls up on a bicycle and says, "Hey! You got any marijuana?"

And I'm like, "What?"

"You got any weed?"

"No, I don't."

"You're a cop, aren't you?" he says.

"No."

"You're a Christian aren't you?"

I'm thinking, *Who is reading who here? I am supposed to be the prophetic evangelist.*

All of a sudden, he said he had to go get high, and I stopped him by saying I had something better than what he was looking for.

"What?"

"God."

I told him I could pray for him and he would feel a touch from God that would be better than a high off weed. He started mocking me, but I prayed anyway. At first, nothing happened, and then I heard the Lord say, *Hit him with the Holy Ghost.* Then I waved my hand past him and the presence of God hit him, and he started to freak out as the presence of God began to overwhelm him. He got on his bicycle and tried to ride away, but he was so drunk in the Spirit that he was fumbling all over the place trying to escape the presence of God. As he attempted to ride away I shouted "Jesus loves you." That experience he will never forget.

We think of the crowd gathered in the upper room in Acts 2 as being drunk in the Spirit when the Holy Spirit baptized them in power and they stumbled and babbled and everyone outside was shocked by their behavior. Or maybe some outside the room also felt the sudden wooziness of the overflow of God's presence coming from the Burning Ones inside.

I was on a boat one time in the Caribbean during a conference at sea, and it was the best place in the world to minister to unbelievers because they cannot get away from you. I was in the bar, hammered in the Spirit (not on alcohol—just filled with the presence of God), and these ladies came up to me and asked what I was drinking. They wondered if the drink in front of me was a Long Island iced tea. I said, "I'm drinking in the Lord."

They were a bit puzzled, so I asked them if they wanted a drink. They said sure. I told them, "This is the deal, though; here's how it works. As I pray for you, you will experience the new wine of Heaven," and I waved my hand in an act of prayer toward one of the women. She started getting hit with God's presence and told me, "It's working." One of her sisters was with her and had been to a church where she must have had some encounters with God, because she said, "Oh my gosh, they are releasing the fear of God. Run!" And they took off.

They can run—but they can't hide. Jesus is still out to seek and save the lost. For some, all it takes is one encounter with God, and their lives are changed forever. Others take a little longer.

It's not just about getting people "drunk in the Spirit." Releasing the presence of God actually releases the manifold wisdom of God. And when the wisdom of God is released, powers and principalities get smacked. Praying for people on the street smacks down the spirits that hold them back from knowing

God. They may feel a bit drunk, but that woozy feeling is actually working something deep in them. Their salvation has begun, the enemy has to loosen its grip, and sickness and disease have to go.

Maria Woodworth-Etter, a revivalist active in the 1800s and early 1900s, walked in this. She would set up tents and hold multi-day revivals. People driving to the meetings would get within a 50-70 mile radius, or cross the line of the city where she was speaking, or drive onto the property, and they would fall out of their buggies drunk. They would get saved and healed on the way down.

This is what God wants to do—and more—by His Spirit, not through our own efforts to torch off a revival, nor through efforts to control the manifestations of revival. We have to cherish revival, even if it looks like Acts 2:13 when those who are filled with the Spirit appeared drunk.

We are going to move into a day when stadiums around the world will be filled with people coming into an encounter with the Word and the Spirit, and thousands will be added to the Church. The apostle Peter said that in the last days God will pour out His Spirit on all flesh:

> ...Your sons and your daughters shall prophesy, your young men shall see visions, your old men shall dream dreams....I will show wonders in heaven above and signs in the earth beneath....whoever calls on the name of the LORD shall be saved (Acts 2:17,19,21).

You are here for a purpose, and your destiny is to release the glory of God in the earth, in every place of influence, and in every place that you have an authority to release it. Not everyone's called to conduct mass crusades or to speak before thousands, but you are called to release the glory in your school, in your workplace, when you are out at the restaurants, in the Starbucks, in the coffee shops; you are called to release the glory of God everywhere you go.

STRANGE FIRE

God's presence has a strange impact on people during times of revival. But Burning Ones must beware not to carry strange fire. Anyone who is filled with the presence of God is a candidate to become a Burning One. But you have to learn how to move in the presence and how to honor the Holy Spirit as you move in His power.

Many years ago, as a young Christian, I had a dream in which God began to speak to me about the religious spirit and the anointing of strange fire. At that time in my life, I was a new Christian who had just come out of a lifestyle of drugs and alcohol and was super zealous for God. In that season of life, I met a bunch of friends who were strange Christians. They were into all kinds of odd things like "smoking Holy Ghost blunts," "toking the ghost," drinking the "Godka of Heaven," and much more. Since I came out of a lifestyle of drugs and alcohol, I could relate with them and thought it was all good.

Before I could wander too far down that road, the Lord spoke to me in a dream. In this dream, I was in a large church, and one of my spiritual fathers (an internationally-known prophet) came to me holding the hand of this strange-looking man who had this strange-looking fire burning all around him. He handed me this man's hand and told me to throw him out of the church, so I took the man by the hand and headed to the back of the church to throw this guy out. As I was walking him to the back door, I noticed that full-on revival begin to break out in this church.

It looked like ocean waves washing through the room, and with each wave, I could see that people were being healed, saved, and delivered. As I was watching this, my heart longed to jump into this move of the Spirit. Suddenly, the man of strange fire, who I was supposed to be ushering out of the church, kicked himself in the face like an idiot. When he did this, whatever fire that was on him jumped on me.

An overwhelming feeling of rebellion came over me. I saw some stones on the ground and picked them up and started throwing them at people who were enjoying the waves of God's glory that were in the room. I especially targeted young kids. And as I was doing it, I laughed hysterically.

When I woke up, I was terrified. I couldn't help but wonder if the dream was telling me that I was in rebellion against God and hurting his kids. Then the voice of the Lord spoke to me in a way that I had never heard before. It seemed to me to be the audible voice of God. He said, "Son, I don't ever want you to smoke a Holy Ghost blunt again because when you do that, you bring the things of God that are holy down to the spirit of this age and make them profane."

As God spoke this to me, all I could do was weep and say I was sorry. The Lord told me that I was forgiven and said not to worry about it because I was innocent in my heart and didn't know any better, like so many others out there who had gotten involved in that deception. Then He told me that He wanted to release revelation to His people about this new manifestation of the religious spirit, and He released the interpretation more fully about my dream.

He said that He is about to release a whole new level of anointing and outpouring of His glory in the days to come, and when it comes, an awesome wave of revival will bring an increase of salvation, healing, and deliverance to the Body of Christ and the world. However, a counterfeit anointing or spirit will also appear. It will be an anti-religious "religious spirit" of strange fire that will hurl stones of offense through odd manifestations.

As God said this to me, I thought about the man of "strange fire" who kicked himself in the face, as well as the stones I threw at the young kids in my dream. Then God went on to tell me that the new manifestation of the religious spirit will have the appearance of being from God, but really will be a spirit of deception. What will look like a spirit of freedom will really be rebellion.

Then He went on to tell me that the assignment of this new religious spirit would be to attack the integrity of the Holy Spirit and cause the fear of God to be taken out of the Church. As a result, the people of God would never enter into a true place of worship and intimacy with Jesus; they would never enter into their God-given destiny, but would waste time rebelling against the Church. He then told me that this spirit was sent from the pits of hell to take out the young ones who have no foundation in the Word or discernment so that they never enter into the things of the Spirit that God is about to release.

After God spoke all of this to me, I began to ask Him where all of this was in the Word. The Holy Spirit led me to the story about Aaron's two sons, Nadab and Abihu, who took their fire pans and flippantly offered strange fire unto the Lord that He did not command, and the Lord consumed them with fire. Let's take a look at this Scripture to learn more.

> Now Nadab and Abihu, the sons of Aaron, took their respective firepans, and after putting fire in them, placed incense on it and offered strange fire before the LORD, which He had not commanded them. And fire came out from the presence of the LORD and consumed them, and they died before the LORD. Then Moses said to Aaron, "It is what the LORD spoke, saying 'By those who come near Me I will be treated as holy, and before all the people I will be honored'"... (Leviticus 10:1-3 NASB).

Though this Scripture sounds harsh, it lines up with all that the Lord was telling me. Nadab and Abihu were mocking a practice that was supposed to be a holy thing unto the Lord, and because of their familiarity and their rebellion toward God, the Lord ended up taking their lives. The sacrifice of fire that the priest was to offer up to God in those days was supposed to be an act of the reverential fear of the Lord as well as worship. Because Nadab and Abihu lacked a reverence for God and His presence, they lost their lives.

This is a picture of what this anti-religious, religious spirit is out to do. Whether people know it or not, when they treat the things of God that are supposed to be holy profanely, they will lose life in the Spirit and will be deceived away from the things of God that are holy. In the end, they will be left with dead religion and will be operating out of the soul realm rather than the Spirit.

God is looking for Burning Ones who will regard the things of His Spirit as holy and not profane the precious things of God, bringing them down to an earthly level. Will you be one who will embrace the purity of God and live in a place of the reverential fear of the Lord?

BURNING ONES AND THE NEW APOSTOLIC MOVE

Now that you can discern the difference between burning with the fire of the Holy Spirit and being consumed by strange fire, it is time for you to take the land that God has destined for you. Burning Ones become so full of God's presence and power that they become the mouthpiece of God. Their words are powerful. They are emerging as true leaders of the next-generation apostolic movement. Are you one who is emerging as a leader in this move of God?

God is birthing a new apostolic, a new generation who will be leaders in the government of God. God will release a new prophetic generation and raise up the next-generation prophets. The new apostles and next-generation international leaders are emerging. These new apostles and prophets will move with real authority, supernaturally endowed power, and functional administrative gifts.

True Leaders Emerging

Things are about to change. We're about to see the glory of God as never before. The fivefold ministry that is spoken of in the Book of Ephesians is about to emerge with a whole new expression for a new generation. The Lord is about to release a distinction in the earth where people will be called out of obscurity into leadership. Some of the greatest leaders that the Body of Christ has yet to see are about to come onto the scene, and God will distinguish between those who are totally committed to Him and those who are not. I believe that we are about to see authentic fivefold ministry gifts emerge in this hour—those who are truly called to be apostles, prophets, evangelists, pastors, and teachers by function. They will be both young and old, but many will be very young in age.

God is about to expose and overturn the systems of people who have held the younger generation down. Many who are calling themselves fathers, but are really big brothers, are trying to use the next generation to build a name for themselves.

Many of those who are calling themselves apostles and prophets, but who are not, will fade away. Right now we are seeing some popular healing evangelists adopt 150 churches and suddenly call themselves apostles. They are not apostles. They are just building networks of churches for financial support. The real deal is coming.

We are also seeing ordinary young believers, accelerated into positions of international ministry, who transcend the functional gifts and release the supernatural miracles of God. They are not recognized as apostles, prophets, or evangelists because it is not yet clear who God has called them to be. But they are moving out as dread champions and are not concerned with a title of human recognition. And as they persist and pursue God, it will become clear who God has ordained for His mantles of apostle and prophet to rest upon.

In the meanwhile, a relational apostolic move is happening that is inter-generational. We all come from somewhere, and we all have mothers and fathers in the faith who teach us from their pulpit, behind the scenes, or through their books, CDs, music, and videos. We're in a huge merging of the generations movement. But there is coming a distinction between the older ones and the younger ones as the torch is being passed from one generation to the next.

How do you recognize a father in the faith? You know what a real father does? He gets behind the sons. Real fathers are honest about all the past failures in their lives, the ways they overcame the enemy, and the victories they celebrate, and they encourage the next generation to go higher than them. They don't stand back and say, "Yeah, you have to earn your way to this one." They get behind you.

The Book of Acts says the promise of the Holy Spirit is available to those who will believe in their children's children. The Bible counsels that a good father leaves an inheritance to his children's children (see Prov. 13:22). A generation is rising that is walking in sonship—as the sons and daughters of God. Are you humble enough to become one?

Are you one who is positioned to receive the torch?

RECEIVING THE TORCH

Here is how you position yourself to become a leader of the coming move of God. You hear the call and leave your cave. You embrace the fires of personal healing and opposition that come against you. You discover what mountain you are called to climb and begin to scale the walls that stand between you and your peak. Along the way, you recognize the power and authority that are your inheritance and are necessary to climb the mountain. You call forth the rain; in a sense, you begin to speak the Word of the Lord with confidence that your Father will back you up because you have first heard what His intent was for you to speak. You become one with Him.

Then you stretch out your hand and receive the torch from the fathers of the previous generation. Let it consume you until you become a Burning One.

DOUBLE PORTION IS PASSED
FROM FATHER TO SON

Many young people carry around a lot of heat on their life; they have a lot of fire and zeal. As soon as they are saved, they begin to think they know it all. Instead, this is what we need to do. We need to humble ourselves, and we need to begin to go to the fathers and mothers and say, "I want what you have. I need the wisdom that you have from the experience of life that you have. I need the wisdom from the things that you've learned and that have happened to you over the time that you've been a Christian so I don't make the same mistakes."

You know what will happen? You will receive a double portion of what they carried in their day. The torch of a Burning One is passed from father to son, the same way it was passed from Elijah to Elisha. It is a torch of the fire of God's presence and favor, power and love, the mantle of authority to lead, and the ability to overcome the works of the enemy and take the land.

God is going to redefine what the double portion looks like in our day. I asked the Lord to reveal to me more about the double portion, and this is what He told me. He said, "Jerame, do you want to know what a double portion is? There's only one way to get it."

I said, "What's that?"

"It's something that's passed down from a true father to a true son. Here's the way it works: It's simply having relationship. It's called a double portion because a true father will give all that he has experienced in life—the good things and the failures. He'll give him the keys that took him many years to learn. And the young ones will receive them if they're walking in humility, and they'll grow, and they'll become double in stature of wisdom and revelation. And then, when the same things that tried to trip their spiritual father and mother up come at them, they won't make the same mistakes. That's what gives them the double portion anointing."

They're doubly strong because they have their father's and mother's love behind them helping them and pushing them forward. We need to begin to embrace each other as the generations. If you don't have spiritual parents in your life, you need to begin to look for the fathers and the mothers who are anointed with wisdom and love and who walk in the gifts of the Spirit.

Also, the fathers and the mothers need to humble themselves and be willing to receive from the younger generation. Many of you in the older generation have been around the block a few times or have been traveling in the wilderness for 40 years. You're coming out. The Lord is bringing you out of the wilderness, and your light is about to shine.

If you are one of the older generation who has been burning out in the wilderness, you need to get some young people to lay hands on you. You need the fire and the zeal that the young generation's carrying. And I'll tell you why; some of you have come into a place where hope deferred has made your heart sick. You've had a vision from God, and it's been so many years that you haven't seen it come to pass that you wonder if you will ever see the things God has promised to you, personally. You may live to see them. If not, you need to begin to believe that your sons and daughters will live the vision that God gave you. And you need to begin to get behind them and impart what you've carried to them.

What I'm doing right now is talking about an emerging army that's coming. It is an army of dread champions. And if you want to be enlisted in the army of God, you need to find fathers and mothers. You're going to have to seek after them. In an army, who are the ones who give direction? It's those who have been promoted to the highest rank—the generals. It's the older ones. It's the ones who have had the most experience. They are the ones who know how to fight, and the weapons of warfare have not changed. The enemy has not grown weaker. The new recruits look different from previous generations. But we are all in this together and need one another.

So, Are You In?

There is a generation of Burning Ones coming who will be a bright and shining lamp for all to see. They will burn with the same love and passion that Jesus burned with to reach the lost and love the unlovely. They will be those who reveal their Father's love to an entire generation by releasing notable, remarkable signs, wonders, and miracles that will result in outpourings of God's Spirit. They will be a company of lovesick worshipers of the King of Glory who won't just talk about God, but will show forth the reality of His Kingdom and power.

They will be those who are as bold as lions, who will carry the nature of the Lion of the tribe of Judah upon their lives. And when they roar, it will be with passion and authority that will displace the powers and principalities in heavenly places and cause strongholds to fall. They also will be used by God to take the mountaintops of influence in society and make Jesus famous once again.

Now is a time of demarcation, and God is looking for those who will go after Him with all of their hearts and sell out to Him for the things of the Kingdom, separating themselves from the mixture of our day, and become fiery hot for Him. Are you willing to press into the fire of God's love until you become one who sees His face and obtains His favor?

Now is the time that the eyes of the Lord are looking all over the earth to show Himself strong on behalf of His people.

The Burning Question

Are you ready to become a dread champion, a Burning One who is willing to pay the price necessary to walk in the greater things of God?

Your Response

_____

_____

_____

_____

_____

_____

_____

_____

_____

_____

_____

_____

_____

_____

_____

_____

_____

_____

_____

A Prayer to Get You There

No reservations, Lord. I'm in! Take me, and let Your fire burn out all that is in me that is not of You. Light me on fire with Your love and power and send me into the world as one who releases Your justice, love, and power. Let me become one of the Burning Ones...the dread champions who move in such an intimacy with You that people are awed by Your presence and healed, delivered, and set free by Your love. I am Yours—completely. Direct my steps, and lead me to those mothers and fathers in the faith who can teach, empower, and release me to become a Burning One, taking the kingdoms of this world and bringing them into an encounter with the King of kings and bringing all things under the Kingdom of God. Bless me, Lord! Send me, Lord! I'm in!

ABOUT JERAME NELSON

CONTACT:

Living At His Feet Ministries
591 Telegraph Canyon Road Suite 705
Chula Vista, CA 91910

Website: www.livingathisfeet.org
Email: admin@livingathisfeet.org
Twitter: @jeramenelson

DESTINY IMAGE PUBLISHERS, INC.

*"Speaking to the Purposes of God for This Generation
and for the Generations to Come."*

VISIT OUR NEW SITE HOME AT
WWW.DESTINYIMAGE.COM

FREE SUBSCRIPTION TO DI NEWSLETTER

Receive free unpublished articles by top DI authors, exclusive

discounts, and free downloads from our best and newest books.

Visit www.destinyimage.com to subscribe.

Write to:	Destiny Image
	P.O. Box 310
	Shippensburg, PA 17257-0310
Call:	1-800-722-6774
Email:	orders@destinyimage.com

For a complete list of our titles or to place an order
online, visit www.destinyimage.com.

FIND US ON FACEBOOK OR FOLLOW US ON TWITTER.

www.facebook.com/destinyimage   facebook
www.twitter.com/destinyimage   twitter